BODY ON THE BEACH

A Rick Dalton Mystery

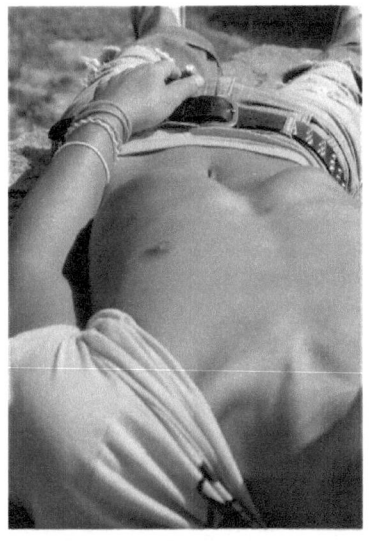

By

Richard D. Clagett

BODY ON THE BEACH
A Rick Dalton Mystery

A work of fiction
ISBN 978-1-304-54322-6

Rick Dalton, former Key West gay guesthouse owner, former London nightclub owner, and former Jamaica gay guest resort owner, is now retired from the business world. He is living in semi-seclusion in an ocean front condo in Florida's fabulous South Beach. He is devoting his full attention to his new soul mate Andres whom he met while soul-searching his chaotic life on a South American holiday. Andres returned with Rick and helped him settle unfinished business in Key West, London, and Jamaica.

Andres is attending Miami-Dade Community College to enrich his command of the English language and to help him decide on a future career and appropriate course of study.

Rick remains at home, relaxing on the beach, enjoying early morning coffee chats on Ocean Drive with his best friend, publisher, and counselor – Bradley, another South Beach condo resident.

Clearly brunching and shopping the trendy spots on Lincoln Road are not enough to satisfy the restless urges of Rick. He yearns to get back into the heat of the action, using his background in amateur sleuthing to stimulate his writing career. Can he resist temptation? I think not, but see for yourself...

Chapter One

He lay there at the edge of the sand, not moving. A little early for sunbathing, I thought, as I finished my first cup of coffee for the day. Blue Mountain, of course, just like back home in Jamaica. I had to meet Bradley at News Café and hurried back inside to get ready. This had become a morning ritual – Bradley and me meeting for breakfast, sharing the latest gossip of South Beach's publishing and modeling world.

"What's up, oh mighty mogul of the magazine world?" I greeted him, as I scooted into the chair by the edge of the walkway.

"Same old thing," Bradley sighed. "Kevin left on an extended photo shoot in St. Martin and me, well, I'm depressed."

"Sales down? Boyfriend not putting out?"

"I think our relationship is dwindling to a standstill. He doesn't need me anymore."

"You made him what he is. You know he'll always be there for you. He loves you," I said consolingly.

"Yeah, but that doesn't warm up my bed."

"How about all those club kids he drags home?"

"Moving right along – when do I get your next manuscript?" he queried.

"Soon as I write it. Not much going on in my life either. Andres is at school most of the day and that leaves me at home on the terrace looking out at the ocean – just waiting."

"For what? Godot?" he smiled. "Get busy; I need another book to publish."

"Maybe I'll start with the 'boy on the beach'. Might be a story there."

"What boy on the beach?"

"He's stretched out on the edge of the sand right below my terrace, shirt pulled up, jeans snugged down low, and all those colored bands around his left wrist…"

"Sounds like you were cruising with your morning coffee. Perhaps I should have found you and Andres a place further inland," he smirked.

"How about you coming over for dinner tonight?" I offered. "Andres and I will fix a special meal just like back at Sugar Hill."

"Changing the subject are we?" he grinned slyly. "I'll be there promptly at six."

I headed across Ocean Drive and onto the beach boardwalk, walking south toward our condo at the edge of Marjorie Stoneman Douglas Park. Perhaps my cute stranger would still be sunning and I could pass close as I entered my building from the beach side.

Yep, he was still there, just where I had spotted him earlier, at the edge of the sand and close to the tall beach grasses just outside our pool deck. Should I go over and offer him a cold drink from upstairs? He might resent me waking him up. Maybe he was sleeping off a hangover from the club scene last night. They get pretty rowdy even on a Sunday night. I chose the safer course and continued on into the building. I'd check up on him later.

I was just finishing up my bill paying on the computer when Andres charged in through the front door.

"Is it that late already?" I mumbled, glancing down at my watch.

"What did you say, sexy guy?" Andres grinned while slipping his arms around me. "You didn't miss me?"

"I always miss you, baby, but I got caught up in a new story for Bradley and I didn't notice it was getting so late."

"I'll be out in a minute," he said, heading for our bedroom. "I need a cool shower and a…"

I missed the rest, but did he mean…? He did!

"Check out that guy down on the beach," I suggested as we came out of our shower room rendezvous in matching white robes. "He's been there all day, in the same place, not moving. He'll be burned to a crisp."

"What guy?" Andres called in from the edge of the terrace. "There's nobody out there."

I walked up behind him, my head resting on his shoulder, and I looked down. The beach was empty.

"You were cruising him all day?" Andres chided.

"You know I don't do that, baby. I'm so in love with you, I never look at another guy that way. It's just that I'm a 'people watcher'. Part of my writer's stock in trade."

The door monitor sounded, announcing Bradley's arrival down in the front lobby of our high tech security building. It saved on the cost of a doorman.

He peered into the camera and said, "Let me in quickly, I need a tall cold drink – and fast!"

"Okay," I chuckled as I released the electronic door locks. "Your icy martini is ready."

"Well, I'll never do that again," he huffed as he stepped from the elevator where I awaited, his drink in my hand.

"What have you done this time?" I chided.

"Walked all the way from West Avenue!"

"Your BMW in the shop again?"

"No, I'm going green this month."

"Things that bad?"

"Just start writing, that's all I'm saying."

"Actually, I started this morning after our brunch."

"What's it about – the 'boy on the beach'?"

Andres looked quizzically over at us.

"Well, not really! It's about a body in the Everglades," I added hastily.

"Do tell, sister," he sighed in contentment as he gulped his drink and slid down onto the cool black leather of our new sofa. "What's the storyline?"

Drug smuggling. Mysterious private airplanes landing in Golden Gate Estates, that southern part of Collier County where nobody can build but all the paved roads are in place. Complete privacy, smooth runway for landing small aircraft."

"Hmm. Sounds like a good start. And then what happens?"

"Read the manuscript. I'm not saying another word," I smirked.

"I'll have another, please," he commanded, holding his glass in the air. "Your dear sister is parched!"

Dinner was much more subdued, as Bradley filled us in about Kevin's ascending modeling career and his own declining magazine and book sales.

"Things couldn't be worse!" he moaned.

"My special dessert will cheer you up," I announced. "Jeremie's white chocolate mousse, just like back home at Sugar Hill."

Bradley and Andres stopped, forks in mid-air, and stared at me.

"Oops, sorry. Our former home in Montego Bay," I meant to say.

"That's better dear. We're counting on you to make a clean break of it all."

"I think Rick still misses his old life," Andres noted sadly, "before me."

"There was no life before you," I consoled, leaving my chair and embracing him warmly. "Just remember our promises and commitments to each other for the LTR."

"LTR?" Bradley quizzed.

"Life time relationship," I stage whispered, as I headed into the kitchen.

By the time drinks were served on the terrace, Courvoisier all around, Bradley had mellowed, Andres had calmed, and I breathed a sigh of relief.

"This coming weekend, if Andres is free of classwork, I'd like to take us all to Naples for the day."

"Italy?" Bradley piped up in surprise.

"Of course not, silly, Collier County, Florida. I'll show you guys the sights and setting of my new book. You'll love the old courthouse in Everglades City, and the one-room post office on Tamiami Trail, if it's still there. The shopping in Old Naples, down on Fifth Street, the seafood restaurants in Tin City…

"I think I'll have to pass," Bradley interjected. "I need to work on getting Kevin back in line."

"That's exactly why I suggested this little jaunt – just the four of us in your BMW; I'll pay for the gas, of course. It worked with Tommie and Philippe when I plotted to get them back together by putting us all on their yacht for the duration of the filming at Sugar Hill."

"I see the machinations of Dolly Levi here," Bradley noted. "Little miss matchmaker!"

We left the plan 'open-ended', so to speak. Who knows what the ensuing week might do to all of us.

We finally ushered Bradley downstairs to a waiting taxi. He was in no condition to walk all the way back to West Avenue, the opposite side of Miami Beach. He was sloshed. I paid the driver.

"He'll never take us to Naples this weekend," I confided to Andres as we rode the elevator back up to our top floor apartment. "The 'open-ended' was to give him a way out. He's really worried about something. I don't know if it's his relationship with Kevin or his financial future."

"How do you know this, Rick?" Andres asked.

"I know him like a 'book'," I laughed. "We've been best friends a very long time and we've been through a great many adventures together."

"You're not disappointed about our trip?"

"No, not really. I didn't want to go anyway. It was just a way for him to be with Kevin in a close personal space for a day. Might do them some good to get away from Miami."

"What about all those places you wanted to see for your book?"

"I haven't written a word. I have no fresh ideas. There is no book. I've got writer's block!"

"At least you still have me," he consoled, with a tug on my arm as he pulled me through the apartment door. "And I'm going to take very good care of you, right now," he grinned slyly as he guided me into the bedroom.

"And Saturday, young man, I'm going to take very good care of you. We're going car shopping!"

Tuesday morning, Andres safely off to school – by bus, until we got that car purchase taken care of, and me off to News Café. Not sure that Bradley would make it after last night's excess consumption of alcohol.

"What ho, Bradley, my best buddy, you're looking wan and pale this morning," I greeted him cheerfully as I slid into my usual chair by the sidewalk.

"I'm supposed to be," he retorted testily, "I am a blonde – a natural one I might add."

We exchanged the usual gossip, me steering clear of any mention of Kevin or the proposed trip, but he eventually got into it anyway.

"He's coming back on tonight's flight from St. Martin or St. John or whichever one of those disciples he's staying at."

"And?"

"We'll probably have to pass on that trip to Naples."

"That's okay, I just put that little trip together for the sake of you and Kevin, and your relationship."

"I thought you wanted to see the scenes of your supposed crime plot."

"No Everglades book, no drug smuggling, no planes in the night landing on deserted highways to nowhere. That was all a fiction to get you guys together and out of town."

"You are working on a book, aren't you?" he asked sharply, with more than a hint of desperation.

"But of course, you know me, always a work in progress. Actually that kind of sums up my whole life – a work in progress," I chuckled.

I opened the notebook I always carry with me, and withdrew a single sheet of paper, scooting it across the table.

"My opening words, just to give you a glimpse of great things to come."

He read my words aloud, but not too loud. There were others sitting around us within earshot.

Boy on the Beach: Chapter One

He lay there all day in the hot sun, never moving. The shadows crept in as the sun fell to the west of the building. Cool breezes came in off the ocean, rustling the tall grasses at the edge of the sand. No one knew who he was. No I.D. They took him away. Another unidentified body now lay at the Miami-Dade county morgue.

"Hmm, very – Hemingway-ish," he murmured. "I like it!"

"Actually I was trying more for Edna Buchanan-ish, my favorite Miami crime writer."

"Just get it done, my dear, I'm counting on you. And…I think I'd better skip tomorrow's brunch and take care of business at home with Kevin."

"Good idea, see you later in the week. Give us a call so we know you two haven't killed each other," I grinned.

We parted ways. Bradley crossing back over Miami Beach on foot to West Avenue and me…hotfooting it down the sandy beach toward home.

The raked sand gave no clue that anyone had been laying in 'the spot' from yesterday. Good thing I took a photo from my upstairs terrace, or I'd be thinking, 'Blow-Up' – the disappearing body in the London park, a film noire by Michelangelo Antonioni, 1966.

(http://youtu.be/ZuO-keZ4KKY) (Check out the movie trailer.)

I hurried upstairs to look at the shots again – just to make sure it wasn't my imagination.

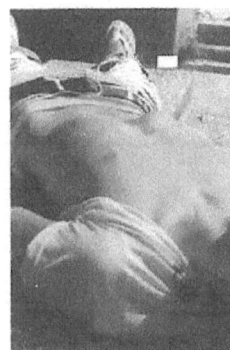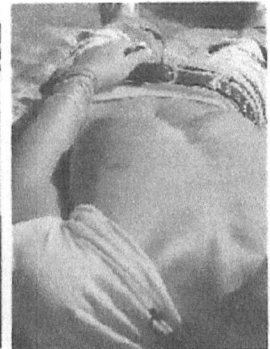

Now that was odd! Something I really hadn't noticed before. His left arm was down at his side in the first photo, up on his waistline in the second, and in the third…well you can see for yourself where it is. At least he wasn't the 'body on the beach'. He was still breathing. Probably waking up after a long nap. I guiltily slid the photos into my notebook with my so-called story. No use stirring up anything on the home front with Andres. Our relationship was new and we needed our 'period of adjustment'.

But from now on, I take my camera and my notebook wherever I go. Never know when a good storyline or photo op comes along.

Saturday morning arrived, no word from Bradley all week. I decided to check up on him before we left for the car dealership.

"Any dead bodies to report?" I joked to Bradley as he came on the line.

"Not yet, but the day is young," he muttered. "And you? How's the story coming?"

"It's coming, but we're taking a break today and going out to look at a car for Andres."

"You don't have a car to go out and look for a car."

"We're going to taxi to Fort Lauderdale," I explained. "Probably drive ourselves back in the new BMW Z-4 I saw online. It's a beauty!"

"Don't be silly, dear one. I need a break right now anyway. I'll drive you two up there, you go shopping, and we'll do lunch after."

"Hmm, sounds like a plan, but lunch is on me if you're driving all the way to Wilton Manors."

"Why so far away?"

"You'll see when we get there."

"Be right over, meet me down front." He clicked off.

"Wow, I guess Bradley is still upset with Kevin. He's in a hurry to dash over here and take us up to Broward County. Very unlike him to be so short-tempered so early in the day."

"What did you say, lover?" Andres called out from the bathroom.

"Nothing, just talking to myself."

"You do a lot of that these days," he commented.

"A gay-friendly auto dealer," I announced as we pulled into the customer parking area of G.L.E. Motors in Wilton Manors. "See the pride flag on display?"

"Yes, my dear, but driving so far for so little selection. There's not a lot to choose from."

"But the selection is late model, luxury and sporty – no SUV's to wade through to get to the good stuff."

We disembarked and wandered through the small array of cars. Not a Z-4 amongst them.

"You guys look around; I'm going into the office." Nice of them not to come charging out into the heat and harassing us like most car dealers. Soft sell I like!

"Where's the red Z-4 you had online?" I asked.

"Sold yesterday. It's being prepped back in the warehouse and going out today," the friendly sales rep announced. "What else can I show you?"

"I guess we'll take a look around," I sighed with disappointment. "We'll come back in if we have any questions." I didn't want any salesman following us around.

"Oh, Rick, I love this one!" Andres called out excitedly as I joined the two of them back outside.

"A Corvette?" I exclaimed.

"It's got black leather seats, the top comes off – it's beautiful!"

I had intended to buy him a red Z-4 like the one we'd left behind in Jamaica, but I had to admit, the 'vette was a black beauty, inside and out.

We decided to lunch at Alibi, a restaurant close by that offered outdoor seating, good food, and…a pride flag! The topic of discussion was Andres' new car, of course.

"You'll have to get your Florida driver license. The international license won't do when we switch the title from my name to your name."

"Oh, I will!" he promised, bubbling over with enthusiasm.

As the sandwiches were served, BLT's all around with cold tea and room for dessert – maybe, Bradley 'fessed up to the reason for his downtrodden demeanor.

"I think Kevin's having an affair!"

Fork in midair, French fry dangling, I sat open-mouthed in surprise.

"Not Kevin, he'd never do anything like that to you," I finally managed.

He's being awfully cozy with one of those models that went on the photo shoot with him. They've been on the phone every night – with the door closed!"

"Just girl talk. You know how closety you were as a teenager. Everything behind closed doors," I offered in explanation.

"You never knew me back then, he's not a teenager, and I was never in the closet!" he exclaimed.

We finished lunch – sans dessert, on a quieter note and returned to the car dealer for Andres' test drive and my financial arrangements. The AMEX card was going to take another big hit. But my baby was worth it.

"There she is. You ever driven a car like this before?" the salesman queried.

"Not exactly," Andres confessed.

"One of my guys will go with you around the neighborhood, make sure you get the feel of it before you make your final decision."

Bradley and I followed the salesman inside while Andres 'hit the road' without me. I had to learn to give him space and show my faith in him if our relationship was going to succeed, unlike the blonde fellow sitting next to me at the sales desk.

"Let me ride with you back to Miami," I whispered to Bradley, "so Andres knows I trust him. You might extend the same courtesy to Kevin."

"I'll give him a couple more days – no pressure. Then we'll talk," he agreed, with a look of resignation. "Uh-oh, here comes your honey, better get the plastic ready."

His look of ecstasy transcended all words; Andres wanted the car – a lot! We signed the papers, paid by debit card, waited for the temporary tag to be attached to the back, and we were off to Miami.

"Thanks a lot, Bradley. We appreciate your help today. Get back to Kevin, but give me a call in the morning. I'll help any way I can," I promised.

I watched him drive away, with a premonition of more serious things on the horizon than Kevin flirting with a fellow model. Something wicked this way comes!

I dashed into the ground floor garage of our building just seconds before the electric gate closed me out. Andres was already parked and waiting, a big grin from ear to ear.

Monday morning, very early, Bradley rang up to confirm our usual weekly brunch date.

"Of course I'll be there," I confirmed. "New week – new gossip."

"And I really have a load of it for you, dear one," he said mysteriously. "See you around eleven-ish."

"Who was that, another boyfriend?" Andres called out from the bedroom.

"Not this early," I called back. "They usually wait until you're safely in school."

"In that case, I'm staying home to keep you very busy with your present LTR guy."

"Who could possibly want anything else when they have a gorgeous guy like you to hug and kiss and…"

"Yeah, that's the part I like best," he grinned, "the and… Save it for me until I get home."

"Why are you leaving this early?"

"I'm still taking the bus until I get some kind of parking pass worked out for the car. It's way too expensive to park downtown in those pay lots by the school."

He was out the door, and I hit the showers.

"So what's the latest with you two?" I began, as I slid into my usual seat at News Café.

"Good morning to you, too. I may have overreacted about Kevin. His friend on the telephone turns out to be one of the guys who went with him to the Caribbean, but is firmly attached to his roommate, if you know what I mean."

"They're lovers."

"Yes. And he's missing. Been missing since before the photo shoot."

"The guy's worried and seeking advice from Kevin? He must be desperate."

"Of course, Kevin recommended you – southeast Florida's greatest amateur sleuth, or so you claim anyway," he said with an impish grin.

"Make that Florida's greatest, and I'll look into it."

"Thanks, Rick; I'll have the guy give you a call with all the details."

"No calls. I don't need any cute guys calling me at home with Andres on the muscle."

"Who said he was cute?"

"Well, he is a model, isn't he? They're all cute or they wouldn't be – models."

"You have a point."

"And I don't want anyone to know where I live either. My telephone number and my house number are off limits to everyone but you and Kevin."

"You could go see him at his place. It's right over on Euclid Avenue, a few blocks from here."

"Me, going to a cute young model's apartment – alone? You don't want me to survive, do you?"

"I forgot, you're the original Mr. 'I can't keep my hands off any cute young guy', and my lover's going to kill me when he finds out. Which they usually do, sooner or later!"

"You call him or have Kevin call him. Say we'll meet in a very public place, like Lummus Park at Twelfth Street. That should be midway for both of us – and in the center of all those people to keep watch over me."

"When?"

"Tomorrow, after I usually leave here, about one o'clock."

"Done."

Chapter Two

It was tomorrow, which is now today, actually. You know what I mean. And he was approaching on one of the busy sidewalks bordering the low coral rock wall of Lummus Park, at Twelfth Street, as planned.

He had an easy stride, but a direct gaze as he approached and said, "You, Rick, the mystery man?"

"I've been called that a few times," I grinned. "You must be Jaime."

"I got a problem, man. Kevin said you might be able to help."

"Let's take a seat over there on a bench, you can fill me in," I suggested.

"This is José," he began, sliding a slightly wrinkled photo out of his jeans pocket. "It's not one of those portfolio pictures, they get touched up too much. It's us at a party last week. I cut me out of it. Better that way."

"Where was the party?" I asked, studying the photo background.

"One o' them hotels up the beach a ways."

"Who else was there that might know him?"

"All of us that was going on the shoot down to the islands."

"You mean the trip to St. Martin that Kevin went on?"

"Yeah, we were going to get our tickets and time schedules."

"How many were there?"

"Eight of us models and the agency guys. They gave us food, drinks, you know – the works."

"You mean they passed out drugs?"

"It was a party, man! Of course!"

No wonder Kevin didn't want to bring Bradley in on this, I thought, as I continued on with an easier line of questioning and an occasional note taking.

"You must have been an athlete before your modeling career," I noted, with an admiring glance. "Football?"

"Yeah, how'd you know?"

"Broad shoulders, massive arms and chest, and…," I stopped before I got in too deep.

"Have been, is right on target. Old football injury cut me out of the action. Standing around in skimpy clothes pays enough," he added. "José hasn't been so lucky – always close but never on target. Thought this time he'd be on the right track. I just don't know what happened, where he disappeared to."

"I'll do my best, nose around, and see what turns up. No guarantees."

"Please help me, Rick. He's my number one guy – I really care about him. Here's my number, anything you need, you just ask. See ya," he said quietly as he stood up and ambled out of sight into the crowd on Ocean Drive.

I sat there on the bench studying the photo a few more minutes. There was something familiar about the face of José. I joined the other crowd on the beach side and made my way south toward home.

Slouched behind my desk, gazing at the computer, I wondered where to start. I couldn't even begin a search without more information. And that leads me right back to Kevin – the only guy out of the eight models at that party that I knew personally. Not 'knew' the way you think! I mean…never mind. Let's keep going. I got on the telephone to Bradley.

"Your soul mate around?" I asked glibly as Bradley picked up.

"I wouldn't go that far, my dear. Let's just call him my roommate at the moment. He's got a lot of explaining to do before this is settled."

"Need to get some background information from him."

"I can fax over his resume and email his portfolio. Will that help?"

"Very funny! He's the only one of the models from that trip that we both know. He might remember something to give me a head start here."

"So you're taking the case of the missing model then?"

"I don't know if we even have 'a case'. And if we do, you're both going to pitch in and help," I warned. "This may be a little out of my league. This Jaime guy should have reported his missing roommate to the police first."

"I'm sure he did, dear one, but a missing 'boyfriend' is not exactly high priority for any police department. Even Miami Beach."

"You've a point, but where is Kevin at this very moment – to get back to the reason for this call in the first place?" I asked in exasperation.

"Don't get testy with me. He's out shopping at the Publix market up the street."

"Will you please have him call me the moment he gets in?'

"On second thought, why don't you and your sweetie come over for cocktails as soon as he gets out of school. Then, if you're real nice to me, I'll fix dinner for all of us."

"Thanks, Bradley. We'll see you about six then?"

"Yes. That should give you a couple of good hours to get busy on that manuscript!" he emphasized.

The manuscript that wasn't, I thought. But...maybe I could put a few words down on paper to mollify Bradley. When your best friend is not only your editor, but also your publisher – you really are between a rock and hard place...most of the time!

Bradley greeted us cheerfully at the door with, "Drinks are being served in the main salon. Go on in guys; be with you in a minute."

"I guess things are back to normal around here," I whispered to Andres, "or Bradley got laid!"

He gave me a startled look.

"Just kidding around, my beautiful boy. Things were getting way too serious around here earlier today when I had Bradley on the phone."

"So, my dears, what's new on the beach side of the island?" Bradley queried, as he wafted in with a tray of drinks in hand.

Andres took over and filled him in on the latest at his college, with his new car, and a few tasty tidbits about me, which I wish he had left out.

"Not to change the subject," I horned in, "but where's my font of information – Mr. Kevin? I've brought my case book to start taking notes."

"He's still in his room, my dear, on the telephone with 'you know who'."

"Oh, I thought he'd be in your room, judging by your jubilant manner this evening."

"We were, but that's another story for another time. Go right on in and start grilling. He's been in there long enough."

"Andres, please look after our host and keep him busy, while I 'grill' the suspect."

"What is the meaning of 'grill'?" he asked innocently, always looking to improve his grasp of the English language.

"It actually has several meanings. In this instance it means I will ask relentless questions about the night of the disappearing model from the only witness I know that was on the scene at the time – Kevin. It can also mean the process of Bradley burning our steaks on his barbeque when he's had too many cocktails," I giggled, as I ducked out of the room.

The evening had mixed results. The dinner was fantastic, as Bradley scored another coup in the kitchen. The information from Kevin was disappointing. Given his condition, the drugs he took, but swore me to secrecy about, had dulled his attention to detail. I had one name – Rafael.

Kevin promised to check him out and call me with the details, if any could be had. Thus ended the evening. We walked back to the apartment. The moon was out in full, the air was fragrant with the salty scent of the sea, and soft breezes blew in from the ocean side. This is indeed paradise.

The meet was set for noon on Friday. Kevin had run through his cell phone contact list and come up with Rafael's name listed under 'Ice'? The guy would look for me at Nexxt Café, a great little spot for lunch on Lincoln Road. I had told Kevin to tell him I would have camera in hand and backpack you know where, to look touristy. He was afraid of being spotted by police – I wonder why! – and would not let Kevin give me his description. Geez, the things I have to go through to help a friend.

The first thing I noticed was the hoodie up over his head, in this heat? The oversized dark sunglasses hid his face. Not exactly inconspicuous!

"You Kevin's buddy?" he asked, sliding into the seat across from me.

"You Rafael?" I shot back.

"Please, no names," he hissed. "Just call me Ice."

"Okay, Ice, you want to order some lunch while we have our little chat, because I'm starved."

We perused the sixteen page menu in silence as I cast an appraising glance at my star witness. Slightly nervous, a little trace of Latino accent, clothing casual but costly. Face very young looking behind the shades, hands smooth and fingernails extremely clean. Not exactly what I had expected from a drug dealer.

"I guess you get paid very well for your services," I ventured, just to get the ball rolling here.

"What do you know about me?" he exploded, dropping the menu.

"Calm down," I soothed. "Kevin just mentioned you seemed to be friends with José and were the supplier of the 'party favors'."

"I'm just a go between, the 'ice messenger'! That's my street name. Somebody lookin' for something, I point 'em in the right direction."

"What was José looking for?"

"Money. This gig wasn't payin' enough."

"You gentlemen ready to order?" the waiter broke in, with a toothy grin and boyish charm. Another would-be model waiting for his lucky break. South Beach was loaded with them. Where did they all come from?

"I'll just have a Coke, no ice," said the Ice man.

"BLT, multi-grain bread, toasted. Hold the fries. I'm on a diet," I joked.

"Anything to drink, sir?"

"Tea, please. With ice. I like ice."

The waiter nodded and left. Ice glanced at me. I stared at Ice.

"It's going to cost," he finally said.

"I'm not looking for a date," I replied. "I just want information."

"I've got expenses."

"I can see that," I remarked, as my eyes ran up and down his designer duds. "Gucci and Guess."

"What do you want to know, Rick?" he asked.

"No names, please!" I shot back. "I'm hiding from the mob!" I kept my grin hidden to myself.

He gave me the longest glance, I guess. I couldn't see much through the tints.

"I just want to find José," I continued. "His boyfriend hasn't seen him since the sendoff party. You were the last to talk to him. Where did *you* send him?"

"The 'go-to' guy set him up with a private gig with a very rich dude. That's all I know."

"That's hardly worth the price of lunch."

"You want to meet the go-to guy, it'll cost you fifty."

A pause, as the waiter served our orders, gave me a chance to think. Was I being conned out of a fifty?

"You take me to him, wait until we're finished talking, that's the deal."

"That'll cost you extra."

Why am I not surprised! The deal was set for later that same afternoon, time and place to be determined by Mr. Go-To.

"How do I reach you?" he asked. "Got a cell?"

"My number is private. What's your number?"

He gave me the necessary digits, the cost of the transaction, and scooted back form the table.

"Call me in one hour, no later," he cautioned as he stood up and walked quickly away, slipping into the swirling crowds of afternoon shoppers.

An hour later, as I was finishing off my double chocolate sundae at a quiet table outside of Ghirardelli's on Lincoln Road, I dialed Mr. Ice. The heck with the diet, the caffeine and the chocolate were two very important ingredients to the true sleuthing process.

"Okay, Ice, when and where?"

Oh no! Not the dark and empty bar on Espanola Way! The scene of a previous encounter with a sleazy informant was not on my list of favorite places. I promised to be there by four and with a hundred dollar bill for Ice.

Ice was waiting for me outside the bar. He'd changed clothes for the occasion. Black jeans, burgundy shirt open to the chest, black leather belt, and the usual Gucci sunglasses.

"You'd go perfect with the black leather upholstery in my car," I joked.

He wasn't smiling, but he was a smash hit anyway with his spiked hair and deep tan. If I wasn't a 'married man' I could sure go for him. Forget I said that – strike that last sentence before Andres reads it.

"Inside, end of the bar," he directed coolly. "I'll be waiting out here."

I walked in alone, blinking in the sudden darkness, adjusting to the doom and gloom of the place. Sure enough, the sleazy informant from a previous caper was waiting at the end of the bar.

"We met somewhere before?" he quizzed, looking at me with suspicion.

"I don't think so. I've never been in this place until now," I lied.

He continued regarding me with uncertainty, but went ahead, "What you lookin' for?"

"Young guy named José you sent on a 'private' job."

"Hey, this is Miami. I know a lot of José's," he laughed.

"He was with the group of models at a party the other night. The ones headed for a photo shoot in St. Martin."

"Oh yeah, the skinny blonde kid. He wasn't right for the job, so I turned him down."

"That's not what I heard. He left with you, was sent out on a date with some rich client. He never came back. His buddy's worried about him. Wants him back home."

"Like I said," did I notice a slight twitch in the eye, "I never set nobody up that night. They was all going down to the island."

"But you do remember talking to him?" I pursued.

"Sure, good lookin' kid, but he didn't look like any model I ever seen. Too skinny, too scared actin'."

"You hear anything, you let Ice know. He'll call me."

Rafael – Ice – had misdirected me on purpose. I turned and walked out of the bar. The place was too creepy for me. Ice was slouched on a chair outside the bar, waiting for his money.

"One of you is lying," I began. "I'd rather think it was that sleaze-bag in the bar and not you. I kind of like you."

Oops, I said too much – again! Sometimes it just slips out. My feelings are going to get me into real trouble one day.

"I'm not that way, Rick, if you know what I mean," he responded.

"You're not gay. That's cool. We can't all be perfect, Ice Man."

"Ice Messenger!" he corrected.

"Whatever! Here's your hundred," I continued, passing over the crisp bill. "We need to talk later. When can we meet again?"

"Eleven tomorrow morning at Big Pink, get a table on the outside. I'll look for you." He slipped into the walkway between two buildings and was gone.

Big Pink was a well-known diner type eatery near my place. Did he know something more about me than I thought? Maybe I was becoming paranoid. Time for a little sanity check. I hurried home to Andres.

"Hey, sexy boy!" I greeted as I pushed open the apartment door.

Andres was clattering away in the kitchen – food prep noises. I was starving. Starving for him, not for food. I'd been around too many weird people for one day.

"Don't bother the chef," he warned, as I slipped my arms around his waist. "Dinner's almost ready. Where have you been all day?"

"Questioning the usual suspects," I said with a grin. "Want to go with me tomorrow, since there's no school on Saturday?"

"Sure, Batman," he kidded, "I'll be Robin tomorrow."

"I guess that's better than being the 'Hardy Boys', they were brothers."

We sat at the dining table, strategically placed at one end of the living space, right next to the glass window wall. My fear of heights was easing; of course this was only the ninth floor, the highest the building had. At fifteen or twenty stories I would be clutching the inside wall.

"This guy we're meeting tomorrow is kind of a shifty character and he knows more than he's telling. I need you to watch his body language as I question him. Maybe you can spot a liar easier than I can. You'll earn your first sleuthing merit badge!"

"What is merit badge, Rick?"

I knew that was coming. I explained.

"So I get one for cooking, one for cleaning, and one for sexual favors?"

"You're learning way too much, way too fast," I grinned.

Big Pink was one block south, two blocks west of our home. We arrived earlier Saturday morning than our appointment time of eleven. I wanted to set the stage for our interview, and go over my plan again with Andres.

"I'll sit across from him, you sit next to him. You can watch his reactions to my questions without being noticed."

"Got it, Rick. I've done this before."

"You have?"

"Our trip when we first met. That long drive to Lima, I didn't take my eyes off you the whole time."

"I thought you were just admiring my appealing profile and my hot body!"

"Hmm," he murmured. "We'll go into that in more detail later."

We ordered iced tea and waited. A cute guy sauntered past our table, looked back, and then broke out in a big grin.

"Andres! What are you doing here?" he teased. "This detective guy been bothering you, too?"

"Rafael, you know Rick?" he asked, stunned.

"Ice?" I gasped. "What the...you two know each other?" I squeaked out.

"I'm known as Rafael south of Fifth Street," he whispered to me.

"We ride the same bus every morning to school," Andres explained. "Rafael's in some of my classes."

"What the...?" Sometimes words elude even me. This was one of them.

Chapter Three

Looking back on it, I think that was the worst attempt to elicit information from an informant that I ever encountered.

"I still think he knows more than he's telling," I mused aloud, for Andres' benefit.

We were having an after dinner drink on our terrace, overlooking the beautiful Atlantic. Andres had prepared another surprisingly good meal, and the wine had been a mystery Merlot picked out of the Publix market's five-dollar-a-bottle sale bin. Now I was into the Bombay Sapphire dry martini mode. Sherlock Holmes had his pipe, I have my martini glass. Whatever works.

"How much do you really know about him?" I queried.

"He's helped me a lot in our English language class," Andres began, "but we don't really hang out together."

"What do you talk about riding home on the bus?" I probed further.

"He talks about the 'hot chicks' in his classes. I talk about my hot boyfriend," he shot back with a grin.

"Anyone I know?"

He slipped his arms around me, resting his head on my shoulder and whispered, "I'll tell you all about him, in the other room."

Well, there goes another bad attempt at interrogation, but you won't hear me complain this time. I followed him into our bedroom. Case officially closed for this evening.

Sunday, August 14, 6:56 AM, more or less. The sun was just edging up out of the clear blue waters of the Atlantic Ocean. I was awake for some unknown reason. Andres was sleeping peacefully at my side, his long chestnut hair softly framing his face. I slipped quietly out of bed and stepped out onto the terrace. This is what it's all about – living on the beach. You don't have to pay a couple hundred thousand dollars to buy a condo, with twelve hundred dollar monthly maintenance fees, to experience this. Just get into your car – early, drive to the beach and behold. It's here for all of us to enjoy, not just the rich and famous, of which I wasn't. At least not the famous part – yet. Well, not really the rich part either. Let's just say I was lucky enough to be comfortable, thanks to book sales and television rights to my gay series on Showcase network. Income from the guest house near Montego Bay helped a little also.

When you leave the beach, stop in at any of the famous eateries along the front terraces and sidewalks of the Art Deco hotels on Ocean Drive. Order Eggs Benedict, a Mimosa or two, sit back and relax with the companion of your choice. Enjoy the good life – without winning the lottery. Go ahead!

Eggs Benedict? Now I was getting hungry. I decided to whip up my favorite version – Eggs Mayflower (from a famous hotel restaurant in Cincinnati, Ohio). Lightly toasted English muffins, topped with crisp bacon strips, eggs sunny side up or over easy, thin slice of tomato, topped with cheddar cheese slices. Leave under the broiler for a few minutes while you warm up an instant Hollandaise sauce, made from the packet or premixed out of a can. Pour sauce over your creation just before serving. Don't forget the Bloody Mary's', or my favorite, Mimosas. Then if anything goes wrong, your guests won't even care with a few drinks in them first. But I digress! Time to wake up my sleeping beauty.

"I'm already awake!" he protested. "What's all that clattering in the kitchen?"

"Breakfast on the terrace, for just you and me."

"Rick, you surprise me. I didn't know you could cook," he complimented as he wolfed down the last morsels of English muffin.

"Let's just say I learned how to 'heat and serve', and leave it at that."

Somebody's cell phone rang from the bedroom, but I ignored it.

"It could be about your missing model case," Andres prompted, "you'd better answer it."

"It's Sunday morning," I moaned. "Everybody should still be sleeping."

"We're not," he smiled. "I'll get it, it could be important."

Groan, groan. I stifled the protest. He was right, of course, he usually is.

"It's Kevin. He needs to speak to you," he said with a satisfied smirk as he handed my cell to me. "Your public must be served."

"Yes, Kev, what is it?" I began, with grave misgivings, as nothing good ever comes from an early Sunday morning telephone call.

I listened with half interest, and then perked up as he gave me the gist of it.

"Oh! Well that's good, I guess. Thanks for the update."

I slid the phone closed and sat processing the new information while Andres scrutinized me from across the dining table.

"It can't be that bad," he said, "unless it's another missing model!"

"Nobody's missing. He came back home. Kevin saw then both together last night at Twist."

"What is Twist?" Andres asked innocently.

"South Beach's premier gay bar. It's over on Washington Avenue just next door to that overpriced diner at Eleventh Street."

"We should go sometime," he offered, somewhat pensively.

"You're bored with your lover already?"

"I have the hottest boy as my LTR, I couldn't ask for any better." He paused for a moment, then continued, "Sometimes I think you need more excitement in your life than I do."

"What brought all this on?" I questioned with slight misgivings.

"I'm away at school all day while you're stuck here in this house all alone and in between books. You need some fresh experiences to get the writing back on track."

"All the hot gay bars we've been to in Lima, and all the hot guys we've run across taught me one thing – you are still my hottest guy. I don't need anyone else."

"You'd better not," he grinned slyly, "but fresh faces and experiences are what you thrive on."

"I think your education is going to your head. Are you taking a psych course in between all those language classes?"

"I don't need a course to know what's going through your mind, Rick. I love you very much, but I do read 'between the lines'."

The most beautiful sunny South Florida mornings can suddenly turn dismal, but not because of distant rumblings of thunder, damp humid breezes pushing in from the west, or threats of rain in the air. Welcome to my life and August in the sub-tropics.

Monday morning brunch at News Café: Bradley pensive and quiet, and me – confused and bewildered.

"What's bothering you, Rick? Fess up! It's me, Bradley, your mother confessor."

"My story just went out the window before it even got started. The missing model was a great beginning, but…"

"You're not telling me all of it. I see more turbulence behind that face."

"I think Andres is bored with our relationship. I guess I'm not exciting enough for him," I galumphed. (Is that even a real word?)

"Explain please, and don't leave anything out!"

I did, tell him everything, that is. Told him the gist of our Sunday morning, but minus the recipe for Eggs Mayflower.

"Is that all that's bothering you? You're too close to the situation. I'm sitting back here, across the table, and even I can spot the problem."

"What are you talking about, Bradley? Another psych major in my family?"

"Andres is afraid he's not giving enough of his time to you because he's in school all day, getting this education you're providing for him. He does have a lot of catching up to do before he enters into college, but you promised to support him through this whole process."

The silence was deafening as he waited for my response.

"You're the one who's bored," he continued, "and Andres can see that plain enough. You're so used to being in the thick of things, life at a frantic pace, like back in Jamaica. Mystery, mayhem, and even murder all around you. Now that you've left all that behind – you don't know what to do with your time."

"Hmm, I see," I murmured, as I pondered his words.

"Get clicking on that keyboard again. Write something, anything. Doesn't have to be this story. There are a million stories out there."

"But…my stories have always been a recounting of my experiences, kind of like journalizing all those strange and amazing things that kept happening to me. Now they've stopped. I can't just make things up. Good writing comes from writing about what you know."

"Well, that's one way, but the imagination is limitless. It can take you anywhere, anytime."

"Give me an example," I teased, I love putting Bradley on the spot.

"I took a creative writing course once…"

"You!" I sputtered. "You've never told me this story before."

"To be a good editor and publisher, it helps to know how to write – even if you don't really do it. I know what's good when I read it and what's trash when I see it." He paused for a moment before adding, with a sly grin, "Which reminds me of that first story you wrote…"

"Don't go there, Bradley," I warned wickedly. "I'd hate to spill hot coffee all over those clean white linen pants you're wearing."

He told me about the writing class, the guest lecturer, Ken Smith, from the UK, a writer of some saucy gay novels based on British ships and sailors. But what I really wanted to get back to was Kevin, so I interrupted again.

"About that roommate of yours – Kevin!" I interjected.

"Was my roommate, but he's back in my good graces again and in my bedroom," he retorted smugly.

"His phone conversation Sunday morning, the one that started this whole disruption of my life, was rather truncated."

"Truncated?" He paused for the dramatic effect. "Where do you come up with all those words? I can't publish 'truncated'. My readers would have to carry a dictionary around with them. I'd never get any of your books sold."

"This is impossible," I said, standing up dramatically. "You keep getting away from the subject matter here."

"Sit down, my dear. Take a deep drink of your chlorinated water and breathe in the gasoline polluted air – slowly. That's better, now go ahead."

"He was his usual 'man of few words', to put it politely. Was there anything he told you that he forgot to tell me about this guy José coming back home to Rafael?"

"Rafael? Who's Rafael?"

"I'm sorry, I meant Jaime."

"No wonder your Andres is worried. Too many guys in your life, can't keep 'em straight, eh?"

"Moving right along…what was the rest of his conversation with those two?"

"He was at Twist, doing his usual networking."

"That's what they're calling it these days?" I smirked.

"Models do that – exposure is the name of the game."

I giggled but refrained from asking about 'over-exposure'. His eyebrows shot upward in a warning look, he knew what I'd been about to say.

"I realize Kevin can't put a whole lot of words together, let alone a string of coherent sentences, but I did marry him for his looks, not his brains."

"Anyway…"

"Yes, he did say more. The two of them had apparently argued over something, and Jaime was physically violent. He gave José a few bruises, among other things, rendering him unfit to do a swimsuit feature for the photo shoot. So José did the next best thing – left the party at the hotel and hooked up with a 'date', and collected his fee. When he realized what he would face when his boyfriend got back from his trip to St. Whatever-Wherever, he was afraid to come home. So, he hid out with a guy he'd met at the party. Funny thing about that," he paused, and then looked over at me very sternly before continuing. "This friend's name just happened to be Rafael! Sound familiar, my dear? What are *you* holding back?"

"Let me tell you about a man called 'Ice'," I began.

I told Bradley all I knew about my mysterious encounters with Rafael - AKA the Ice Messenger, the Go-To man, and Andres friendship with Rafael.

"Well, all 'Icy' matters aside, you still have your story."

"What story?"

"Domestic abuse, a hot topic. Even in the gay community it's just as devastating to the victims as it is in that 'other' world."

"But there's no murder, no suicide, no accident like falling off a boat. In short, no reason for 'The Body on the Beach'."

"Therein lays your problem," Bradley stated calmly, "that opening paragraph of the story you presented to me. It begins with a dead body, and now you feel like this story doesn't match the ending you pre-wrote. You put the cart before the horse, so to speak."

He watched me intently as I struggled with my thoughts.

"Start over," he advised. "You have a different story to write now, things that need to be said."

We parted at noon and I headed south on Ocean Drive to the condo, Bradley's words rolling around in my head. It did not go unnoticed that he was trying to keep me busy and out of trouble. He wanted me to start a series of articles for his gay magazine, 'Southern Exposure', on 'gay lifestyle'. It would deal with problems that come up during a committed relationship. Things that we were never taught how to handle as members of that 'ten percent' of the world's population.

I started researching the topic of 'Domestic Abuse' on my computer as soon as I got inside. It's amazing the amount of information that's available online when you start 'googling'. The afternoon passed quickly.

"Rick, you need to call Rafael, please," Andres announced breathlessly as he rushed through the front door.

"He's finally ready to tell all, is he?" I said mysteriously, twirling an imaginary mustache, like the villains in the old movies. Actually I do have a mustache, but not long enough to twirl.

"He wouldn't tell me anything and he wasn't on the bus this morning."

"And you know he wanted me to call him – how?" I asked with misgivings.

"He just called me a few minutes ago as I was walking down from the bus stop."

"You gave him your cell number?" I asked incredulously.

The pause was deafening

"A guy that sells drugs and pimps male hustlers? You want your number coming up when he's arrested someday and they search his cell for contacts?"

He looked completely crestfallen, and I was immediately sorry. I went to him, drew him into my arms and apologized profusely.

"I love you so much, and I don't want anything to cloud our relationship. I promise to trust you to make your own decisions from now on."

Andres deserved only the very best from me at all times.

"In my defense, Rick, Rafael was only a classmate to me. I didn't know him as an iced man."

"Close enough!" I chuckled. "You're absolutely right and I'll make amends now."

The return call to Rafael was soon forgotten as Andres and I headed into our bedroom and closed the door. Don't ask me why we close the door. Old habits, I guess.

The Ice Man didn't forget us, however, as his call came through just when we were sitting down to eat dinner. Of course it was after nine o'clock in the evening, but Andres had insisted that I do a lot of 'amending'. No complaints from me!

"It's Rafael," he confirmed, handing his cell phone to me.

"Sorry, I couldn't call back. I was very busy this afternoon."

"I need your help, Rick," he insisted.

"*You* need *my* help? That's a twist, no pun intended."

"José is here with me. He's been roughed up by his roommate again."

"Hey, leave me out of it," I began, and then it hit home – my magazine article. "On second thought, I need to interview him."

"He can't stay here. My friend is coming back this evening. He doesn't allow strangers in his apartment when he's out of town."

"Well, we don't have a guest room. So find somewhere else for him to stay, but I need to talk to him first."

"Meet us at South Pointe Park in one hour!" he said as he hung up on me.

Turning to Andres with a most mournful expression, I explained the unheard of part of the phone call and ended with, "Your friend Rafael is getting us in way too deep."

"I'll go with you for backup," he said with a grin.

"Shall I call you Robin or Tonto?"

"What is Tonto, Rick?"

"Way before your time, I'll explain later."

The beach walkway meandered south past the back of our building, ending up at South Pointe Park. We traversed the distance in fifteen minutes at a brisk pace.

Two silhouettes stood down by the edge of the channel for the cruise ships. They were back lit by the bright glow of lights on Fisher Island at the far side of the channel. Strong winds blew in across the water from the ocean on our left.

"Must be them, who else would come out here on at ten o'clock in the dark? On second thought…it is a beautiful night for lovers," I murmured as I glanced up at the clear starry skies above.

We strode toward them with trepidation. What was I getting us into?

"I don't see any bruises, cuts, or abrasions," I declared upon closer examination as they turned toward us.

"Models don't hit other models in the face, an unwritten code," Rafael explained. "There are other ways, other places to inflict pain."

José was slim, tanned, and beautiful in a boyish sort of way. His blonde crew-cut hair was brushed back in the spiky mode. He definitely looked familiar. He *was* 'the body on the beach'!

"I don't know if Rafael explained," I said, turning toward José, "but I need information."

"Not now, Rick!" Rafael broke in. "Just give him a place to stay for one night. My friend leaves again tomorrow and José can come back."

Andres placed his hand on my arm and spoke out, "It's okay with us, for one night. He can sleep in the study."

When I told Andres earlier that I would support his decision making, I didn't have 'bringing home cute young models' in mind.

"Thanks, guys," Rafael said quickly as he turned to leave. "See you on the bus in the morning," he nodded to Andres.

We trudged the pathway back up the beach in relative silence. Attempts at conversation were useless. José was lost in his own world at the moment.

"Here's the kitchen," I explained to José as we trooped into our condo. "You get hungry during the night, help yourself to anything in the refrigerator."

Andres showed him the bathroom with fresh clean towels and beach robes stacked neatly in the cupboard.

"I'll unfold the hideaway in the den," I offered, leaving the two of them back out on the terrace.

"Strangely quiet, our young guest," I noted as Andres closed us in our bedroom. "He's either traumatized or high on something."

"Thanks, Rick," Andres said simply. "You did the right thing."

"I hope so. Maybe tomorrow we can get to the bottom of it all. A little interview, then he's out the door."

We snuggled together in the gathering silence. Andres fell asleep almost instantly, while I lay awake, pondering over our strange house guest.

Early morning found me still asleep, probably from too much pondering, and Andres was up and about.

"Rick, wake up." he whispered softly, while shaking me gently. "He's gone."

"Gone?" I muttered drowsily, "Gone where?"

He handed me a penciled note found on the dining table.

Thank you, guys.
Going back home to straten (sic) things out.

"That's it, after all he's been through, and he's going back to the lion's den?"

"The power of love, I guess," Andres noted.

"I think it's more like – 'the prisoner of love'. I've been there myself, and I don't recommend it!"

Andres looked at me strangely.

"That time Sylvain lived with me, I got beat up more than once and kept taking it instead of throwing him out," I finished lamely.

The cell phone chose that moment to ring, thus saving me further embarrassing explanation.

"It's Bradley for you," Andres explained, handing the offending instrument to me.

"Saved by the bell?" I smiled up at him.

"You can tell me more about your POW days after I get back this afternoon," Andres smirked as he headed for the shower.

"To what do I owe this dubious pleasure?" I announced over the phone.

"A change in plans," Bradley said simply. "I need your help."

"Last time I heard that expression, it led to a mysterious intrigue in the dead of night on a deserted beach with a dead body come back to life."

"What are you talking about?"

"Tell you later, Bradley, now what's the change?"

"Instead of our usual at News Café, meet me at McDonalds, Lincoln Road and Washington Avenue."

"Are we on a budget cut, or is it a cute new trainee behind the counter?"

"See you at ten o'clock," he ordered before hanging up on me.

"I hate when people do that!" I muttered.

"You say something, Rick?" Andres asked, stepping out from the bathroom, towel in hand.

"Just the usual, talking to myself."

"Perhaps we should think about getting you a pet."

Walking from home to Lincoln Road at Washington was about two miles, give or take a heart attack or two. Good thing it was mid-morning, but it could have been worse, it could have been raining.

"You walked?" Bradley queried, as I stepped into the ice cold air of McDonalds.

"Does it show?" I grinned, wiping my brow with a shred proof napkin.

"Here, this'll perk you right up," he said offering me a café con leche.

"Gee, Bradley, you shouldn't have."

"I had coupons, drink up," he ordered as he ushered me back outside.

"Where are we headed?"

"To your new office. Follow me."

We went around the corner of the same building and into the foyer off the Lincoln Road side. He pointed out the building's directory on the wall next to the elevator. At the suite number he indicated was the name, Model Solutions.

"What is this place?"

"My old modeling agency which we are gearing back up for business."

"Things are that bad at the magazine?"

"Let's just say we're expanding our realm of influence."

The office we entered on the second floor was set up as a reception area with three private office/conference rooms behind. Décor, mid-century modern, as befits a place in the deco world of Lincoln Road.

"The receptionist, Isabel, gets in at one and leaves at five. She's in school at U. of M. studying business administration. Your job, if you accept it, is to man the phones, scan the mail, and take applications."

"You're offering me a job?" I exclaimed, in bewilderment.

"Nine to one only, to fill in your 'dead space' until your beloved Andres gets home from school."

"But my writing…?"

"Believe me, your mornings will be very empty here, just bring your laptop and write away."

The pause of silence, as we stared at each other.

"And it pays," he grinned at my astonishment

"I'll bet your magazine office is right down the hall, isn't it?"

"Always has been."

"A controlled environment, so you can keep tabs on my progress with the book," I noted with dawning revelation.

"And because I really do need your help on this project. You have a keen sense of business organization, with the guest house experience."

"But I don't know anything about modeling, contracts, and whatever else goes into it."

"Not to worry, we'll go over it tomorrow."

I left in a daze, trying to grasp the enormity of the changes in my life about to occur. A return walk down Washington Avenue to Fifth Street was just the calming antidote. Guess, Armani, Ralph Lauren, Benetton, Tommy Hilfiger – they were all there, right in a row. And I stopped in at each and every one of them. My credit card remained in my pocket. I was not shopping, I was soaking up the air of current fashion.

I arrived home before Andres, as it should be. I never wanted him to walk into an empty house again, wondering where I was. Our custom had been to have a late lunch or an early dinner, depending on the stress level of the day. I began the lunch preparation. We needed this time together.

"I told Rafael on the bus about José leaving early," Andres began as we sat down to my gourmet lunch prep of BLT's on whole grain toast.

"And…?"

"He was just like you, surprised!"

"Out of our hands now, I wish him luck."

"Are you having a change of heart about helping José, or is something else going on here?" he asked with a knowing expression.

"Can't keep a secret from you," I chuckled. "It's Bradley. He's trying to put me to work in his office to keep me busy while I look for another story to write."

"The magazine?"

"No, the modeling agency he let sit dormant for a few years."

"Uh-oh, I smell trouble!"

"Now Andres, don't get the wrong idea. I won't be sitting around all day interviewing hot young guys that want to be stars. It's just answering the telephone, opening the mail, filing, stuff like that. He wants to keep his eye on me so I keep on writing. Nine to one every day. I'll be back home before you."

"Hmm."

"If you don't want me to work there, I won't. It's up to you."

He came around the table, put his arms around me, and gave me a great big hug.

"Of course you're going to take the job. I'm just giving you a hard time so you know how much I really love you, Rick."

"Thanks, baby, I needed that."

Chapter Four

To preserve my fabulous new wardrobe, I drove Andres' car to work and parked at the Lincoln Road garage. No perspiration, no wrinkles – well, maybe a few, from being jammed into the black leather seat of the Corvette.

Bradley greeted me as I stepped into the office, Starbucks' caramel macchiato flavored coffees resting on the desk.

"Thought you could use the good stuff for your first day, just don't get used to it."

"With a boss like you, I'll be lucky to get bottled water!" I shot back.

"Not even!" he retorted, "and these are your new business cards."

"Address, fax, and telephone numbers are on the back. Hand them out wherever you go. Never know 'where lurks the next hidden talent'."

For the next two hours we went over composite cards, portfolios, files, contracts, model releases, and indexes of photographers, art directors et cetera. I was really deep in the woods here – make that 'lost at sea', being this close to the Atlantic!

"You can start on that computer in the middle office. Anything you write for your article or book, you can zip file and email to yourself, since I see you forgot your laptop."

He breezed over to the door, turned and said, "I'll be back at one o'clock to introduce you to the next shift – Isabel. Tata!" And he was gone.

I'd been living in the quiet that comes with anonymity, and now I was thrust into the heat of the action, or so it would seem.

"Hey, Rick, I'm home. Any scratches on my car?"

"Just the left front fender! But I did stop and pick it up and slid it into the back of the car. We'll have it reattached in the morning."

The look of disbelief on his face was priceless! I gave him a great big hug and added, "Just kidding. And I think we should leave it in the garage from now on. Way too many cars out there getting in my path."

"You're not going to walk all that distance?"

"I found out that the bus runs from Fifth Street all the way north past Lincoln Road, and I'll try it tomorrow."

"I'll walk you to the bus stop in the morning and show you how it works," he grinned. "A guy with a Bentley and a 'Z' has probably never ridden with the rest of us common people."

"Touché, my dear. How was your day?"

"I won't even ask what that word means," he shot back.

We moved out on to the terrace, drinks in hand – martini for me, iced tea for the kid. He told me about Rafael, nothing new on that front. I told him about the office, plenty new, at least for me.

"Just what is the difference between a laptop, notebook, tablet, kindle, and I-pad? That's the confusing part. The rest of the office I can handle."

"They have all those things in the office?"

"At the very least! All I wanted to do was write and I forgot to take my own computer."

He promised to help me organize my morning, pack my lunch, and send me back out into the world with my own laptop safely stowed in its carrying case, which I had forgotten I had.

"Now we've settle that, let's get back to José."

"Really stuck on that guy, aren't you?" Andres mused.

"Stuck on the story. I can't write what I don't know. Interviews with someone in a dangerous relationship like those two guys have would go a long way toward getting me started again."

"Should I call Rafael for you?" he offered.

"I'd rather leave him out of it. He's want paid for anything he told me."

"Why not call Kevin, get him to call José for you?"

"Brilliant! And beautiful! What more could I ask for?"

"Who, me or Kevin?"

I didn't answer that – verbally, anyway. A demonstration is worth a hundred word explanation. We postponed dinner for quite a while.

Much Later:

The call to Kevin was made. He didn't have a private cell number for José, but he promised to call Jaime and have him stop by the modeling office with the pretext of registering his composite card with us.

"Very enterprising for Kevin to think of that," I said aloud for Andres' benefit, and then explained it all.

"What is a composite card?" he asked, naturally enough.

"It seems to be a condensed version of a model's portfolio with five photos printed out on a six by eight inch index card for quick reference. I think."

And the next morning:

Me and my brown bag (lunch) and black travel case (laptop) were escorted by Andres to Fifth and Washington – my departure point for the office. I felt like a kid with his mother watching him get on the bus for his first day at school. I chose to leave the power suit behind today and wear a casual look. Andres was my wardrobe advisor. He insisted on corporate casual, at the very least. Blue Ralph Lauren button down collar shirt, light tan Polo chinos, Bass Weejuns in burgundy and with a tassel.

It felt odd, Andres and I leaving at the same time, but in opposite directions. I don't know what I'd ever do without him.

"What, no coffee?" I remarked upon stepping into the Model Solutions office with both bags in hand.

"I've taken the liberty of purchasing a one-cup-at-a-time Keurig machine, just for you, my dear one," Bradley announced. "That way you'll always have fresh and the flavor of your choice."

"Bradley, you shouldn't have!"

"I know. It cost a lot, but then, with the production you'll be putting out," with that he glanced at my laptop, "it'll be worth it."

"And the model of the day should be arriving soon," I said mysteriously. "Your boyfriend sent out a few feelers to his cronies, and I expect Jaime at the very least."

"Oh, that one!" he remarked.

"Good for you and priceless for my story, I mean – article."

"Don't expect too much out of him, it's the other one you need to get next to."

"Oh, I've already been next to him," I teased. "He spent the night at our apartment two days ago."

"I thought you didn't take your work home with you?"

"He was actually forced on us, but that's a story for later. I'd better get to work before the boss starts yelling at me," I chuckled.

"I'll check in with you a one o'clock when Isabel gets here," he promised as he hurried out the door.

I think I spooked him really good, about our house guest.

Jaime showed up at noon, not a great deal of time to get into his mind. I tried my best.

"This looks really good," I complimented, holding the comp card in my hand. "Great face shot!"

We chatted on for a few minutes before I could get around to my original purpose. He mustn't know that José had been found – and stayed in our home, no less.

"Sorry I couldn't find José for you, but I called all my informants. Not a word on the street about him."

"He's away on a photo shoot," Jamie said quietly. "I got his schedule mixed up. He called, coming back in a few days," he finished lamely. "Sorry for your trouble, Rick."

"I'm glad the mystery is solved," I said casually. "Have him stop in with his composite when he gets back, I'd like to meet hm."

"Yeah, sure thing, Rick. See ya'," he added quickly as he scooted out the door.

Guess this is my day for scaring everyone away, I thought. I returned to my writing. Good thing, because Bradley walked in just moments after Jaime left.

"Did he show?"

I slid the comp card across the desk.

"Well?"

"He's lying through his teeth. He couldn't get out the door fast enough when we got around to my questions."

"You do have that effect on people," he grinned.

Much later...me at home staring out across the calm waters, thinking, plotting, planning my next move, but to no avail. Andres was whipping up one of his new recipes in the kitchen. I finally gave in to his original suggestion of yesterday.

"Could you call Rafael for me, after dinner of course?" I begged. "He's the only lead we have left."

"Now you're glad we have his number, eh?"

"I've got his number all right – preceded by dollar signs!"

The dinner was magnificent, veal medallions, fresh asparagus with a light cream sauce, roasted new whole potatoes, hot rolls with better, and a light rosé, not from Publix. Dessert was saved for later, for the arrival of Rafael. I know what you're thinking, that I vowed nobody would ever have our telephone numbers or address except Bradley and Kevin. This was an emergency however, and since Rafael wouldn't let us know where he lived, and José already knew where we lived, the secret was out, so to speak.

The buzzing at the downstairs security door announced his arrival. I was ready to pay a token fee for his information if necessary, but I hoped we were beyond that level now. A few drinks might ease the way.

"Sorry to bring you out tonight, Rafael, but I need some help here."

We were enjoying the light breeze from the terrace, martini for me, iced tea for the two students. Rafael was as careful as Andres, not to drink on a school night.

"I didn't get a chance to pump our houseguest the other night. He was spaced out or something. Went right to his room and then disappeared in the AM before either of us was up."

"He didn't take anything, did he?" Rafael asked with a worried look.

"Why would he do that? What did you forget to tell us about him?"

"This is just between the three of us. He's got a real bad habit."

"Kleptomania?"

"I don't know what that means, but he's hooked on heroin."

"Ah!" was all I could say. I hadn't seriously considered drug addiction. Now things were looking a little clearer. "So how about the bruises he was supposed to have?"

"I've seen them. Like I told you guys, models don't do the face."

"So you still think Jaime is responsible for all of it?"

"Who else?" he nodded glumly. "The guy's on a power trip and taking it out on José."

"Or José's been picking up his product in the wrong part of town. White guys with his looks sometimes get beaten and robbed, sniffing around Overtown at night."

Rafael stared at me before continuing, "What do you know about that area?"

"Only what I read in the crime columns. My explorations stop at the railroad tracks." (I was referring to the little-used but about to be revamped Florida East Coast Railroad line running alongside NW Second Avenue in Miami – a dividing line between safe and unsafe neighborhoods.)

"I know he doesn't go over there!" Rafael insisted.

"Because…you're his supplier?" I ventured.

"No way, man! I don't sell drugs. I hook up guys with dates, yes. What they do on those dates is not my problem."

"A regular 'Welcome Wagon' for needy guys, eh?"

He sat there glumly staring – at me.

"I thought José was your friend, that you cared about him," I reasoned in a softer tone.

I took a short break to the kitchen, looking for the Bombay Sapphire. I needed to lay off questioning Rafael for a while. He might just storm out and leave me nothing.

Andres joined me, and started prepping his dessert, a dark chocolate something or other, but who doesn't love chocolate?

"I'd go easy on him," he said quietly. "He's really a good guy."

"Yeah, he does seem to care about his friends." I paused before adding, "His friendship…it means a lot to you doesn't it?"

"He's the only one I really know here in Miami, except you of course." Then he grinned widely. "You're my very best friend, my lover, my life."

It hit me like a bolt of lightning. I was about to trash his one and only friend, right in front of him, and I couldn't go through with it.

I backed off. There were other ways to get to Rafael without hurting the one I love.

We enjoyed our chocolate something with quiet conversation on the terrace as the star-filled sky reflected back from the gently flowing tides of the great Atlantic.

Later, I walked Rafael down the hall to the elevator, hoping for a tidbit or a clue – and I got it!

"He'll be on the Tropicana this weekend, on a cruise to Bimini. That's all I know."

The doors slid closed, sending my informant down to the lobby before I could question further.

Thursday evening after a pleasant dinner with Bradley and Kevin at their bayside condo, I turned to Andres and whispered, "Are you up for a weekend trip to Bimini?"

"A honeymoon cruise?" he grinned conspiratorially.

"I wish!" I groaned. "A spying mission. We'll be tailing our elusive houseguest – José."

"Where is this Bimini?" he whispered back.

"Western edge of the Bahamas, about fifty miles, gives or take." I let that sink in before adding, "We need to take Bradley and Kevin for backup."

"There goes the honeymoon," he sighed wistfully.

"I'll make it up to you very soon, I promise!"

"A lot of private gossip going on in that corner?" Bradley queried as he wafted into the living room with a silver tray of after dinner brandies, Courvoisier of course.

"Just getting Andres' approval for a little rendezvous with our destiny," I answered jauntily.

"Oh dear, the cryptic phrases again," he huffed.

"Actually, it's about the first case for our newly formed group, the 'South Beach Boyz'! Successor to our old 'Sugar Hill Gang' in Jamaica," I said with a grin.

Chapter Five

We stood on the afterdeck of the M.V.Tropicana cruise ship, bound for Bimini, as we glanced back at the receding lights of Miami. Andres and I snuggled together in the cool winds of the evening, wondering why we were here.

Bradley and Kevin were below deck, artfully disguised as 'sugar daddy' and 'sweet young thing of the moment', as they flitted through the casino looking for our target.

Just then a figure emerged from the shadows surrounding the edge of the deserted pool. "You guys lookin' for me?" It was José!

"Well, we were just…" I hesitated, but Andres came to the rescue.

"…on a belated honeymoon," he finished for me.

"Kevin and his friend? They on a 'honeymoon', too?"

Busted! He was a lot more observant than I'd guessed.

"And what brings you to this 'ship of fools' headed for Bimini?" I countered.

"A photo shoot on the beach. I missed the last one and I really need the money. So, here I am. See you on the sand, guys," he shot back as he turned and blended into the blackness.

We spotted Bradley and Kevin well ahead of us in the Sunday morning brunch line. Bradley glanced back and motioned me forward, but I shook my head, not wishing to be accused of cutting ahead of the others in line.

I nodded toward the tables, indicating my desire to join them there. Since our cover was already blown with José, we might as well get back together and plan our next move.

"He's here on a job," I began as I slid into the chair across from Kevin. "Did you know about any photo shoots coming up?"

"Not me," Kevin mumbled, shoveling a forkful of pancakes into his mouth, the syrup dripping down his chin.

"Nor me," Bradley grumbled as he shot a disdainful look at his lover.

"He says he'll be out on the beach," I offered. "We need to scour the sands and verify his story.

"I still don't know why, exactly, that we're here," Bradley muttered.

"That's the same thing we were thinking last night," I agreed, as I glanced over to Andres, "but Rafael advised that José would be on the boat to Bimini, so here we are!"

"And just what are we looking for?" Bradley persisted.

"Maybe a hook-up with a 'rough trade' boyfriend. Perhaps a drug deal. I just don't know." I looked thoughtfully around the room for a moment, not seeing José anywhere, and continued, "Soon as we're done here, let's disembark, split up, and comb the beach."

"Disembark?" Bradley muttered, shaking his head.

"That *is* what they call it," I huffed in my own defense. "You're certainly in a foul mood this morning."

"Thanks to you and this trip to nowhere," Bradley scolded, "I lost five hundred dollars at the blackjack table!"

"Five hundred dollars! Are you out of your mind? Who said you should gamble?"

"We couldn't keep cruising around the casino looking for your friend without doing something. It would look too suspicious."

"Perhaps they'll put up a plaque in your honor at that table, 'Sucker of the Evening'," I shot back

"Don't worry, it's coming out of your next paycheck," he warned.

We had agreed to meet up at the end of the pier after we repaired to our separate cabins and changed into beach wear.

"Oh, my," I snickered, as Bradley came marching into view wearing a floppy straw hat, oversize sunglasses, and white linen slacks, "he looks just like Nathan Lane in 'The Birdcage'!"

Before Andres could ask me what I meant, Bradley stormed up and said, "I'm in disguise, so you can just forget the commentary."

"My lips are sealed," I grinned back. "Welcome to Alice Town!"

The day was gone all too quickly. Bradley and Kevin had rented a golf cart (go figure!) and toured all seven miles up to the tip of North Bimini. Andres and I had chosen another course by checking local lodgings for news of photo shoots that might be in progress anywhere on the island.

"Not exactly Key West," Bradley sighed as he and Kevin joined us at our table in a dockside eatery.

"Not Fire Island either," I replied glumly. "Entirely too quiet!"

"But Hemingway found it inspiring," Bradley noted. "He wrote one of his better novels while he was living right here – 'Islands in the Stream'."

"And your point is?" I retorted.

"Are you taking notes for *your* book?"

The arrival of a large fishing boat with José standing on the deck cut short our repartee. As it was being tied up to the fishing pier, he jumped down, a canvas bag in each hand, and headed our way.

"Should we invite him to join us for a drink?" I offered.

The three of them stared at me.

"What better way to find out what's really going down around here!"

"Well, that's progress, I guess," I announced, rejoining the expectant three waiting at my table. "He won't come inside now, but wants to talk privately later back onboard."

"He did look a whiter shade of pale," Bradley noted. "You must have said something that scared him."

"I merely asked what was in those two tote bags, they didn't look like clothing or camera equipment to me."

We agreed to talk later among ourselves, over drinks in the ship's lounge.

"Andres and I are going to take a brief walk down to the end of the wharf," I announced with a wink at my partner. "See you guys on the ship in one hour."

"What are you up to, Rick?" Andres whispered as we slipped out the door.

"A little photo shoot of our own. You did bring your new camera I hope?"

The guys were waiting for us in the bar when we rejoined the cruise ship.

"The 'South Beach Boyz' have a real mystery on our hands now," I announced. "That fishing boat was carrying more than a model for a magazine ad. José had said they picked up a couple of packages in Grand Bahamas Island."

"No wonder we couldn't find him on the beach," Bradley broke in, "he's been gone all day!"

"And the packages they picked up were in his canvas totes!" I continued. "Andres and I strolled down the wharf and videotaped all the boats in dock. Got names and deck crew photos – the works."

"Why go to all that trouble if all you wanted was a shot of that big one he came in on?" Bradley queried.

"Cover for José, so we looked like a couple of tourists asking about fishing trips out on the water. He was very nervous about anyone seeing him speak to me."

The drinks arrived. I swirled my lemon twist through the straight-up Bombay Sapphire martini before continuing.

"I told him we'd meet up on deck tonight, in the shadows."

"All of us?" Bradley questioned.

"Just Andres and me…," I glanced over at my better half, "…he'll watch my back while you two act innocent as you stroll through the casino again, but *no* gambling this time!

Buffet Dinner was served at seven o'clock on deck to catch the falling rays of sunset dancing magically across the waters as the boat steamed westward toward Miami. We all ate sparingly of the rich foods spread out before us. There was important work to be done tonight. Andres and I moved aft to linger by the pool, Bradley and Kevin sauntered back inside to observe the casino action.

"Does this remind you of anything?" I whispered as I drew Andres close and leaned back against the deck railing.

"That night on the gambling boat in Miami," he grinned. "That Brooklyn lady thought you were Ricky Martin."

"More than that. It was the first night we spoke about our future. You gave me parameters for our relationship – no treating you like a trophy, no spoiling you, no showing off to my rich friends. Now you know the truth, I don't have any rich friends. It's just you and me together for the LTR."

We kissed lightly as I held him in my arms, the growing darkness covering our intentions.

"And I still want to spoil you," I whispered. "That's what I live for."

"I thought it was my sexy body!" he grinned as he guided my hands slowly downward, pressing harder into me.

"Sorry to interrupt, guys." It was José, slipping out of the shadows again. "About those packages – they're gone!"

It took a minute to refocus my thoughts, what did he mean gone?

"They were stolen?"

"I was ordered to leave them in my room and take a walk around the ship. For about an hour. I came back. They were not in my room."

"Who told you all this?"

"It's a long story."

"Don't worry, we have all night." I glanced at Andres before offering, "Come back to our cabin where we can talk in private."

We guided ourselves through the crowds, waiting to line up for the usual questions and scrutiny by the U.S.Customs officials. Standard fare in these days of world unrest. A few simple questions about purchases in Bimini, a calculating glance at the eyes, an observation of body language – it told the officers all they needed to know. Most of us were passed right on through to the welcoming Port of Miami. A few were singled out for luggage search, but not us.

We reclaimed the car from the terminal parking garage, Bradley's BMW. Andres and I settled in the back as Bradley with Kevin in the front maneuvered our way back out to Biscayne Boulevard in downtown Miami. Just a short hop across the MacArthur Causeway and we were home, safe and sound, in beautiful South Beach.

"Well that was fun," Bradley announced sarcastically as he pulled up in front of our building on Ocean Drive. "We'll have to do it again real soon."

"At least I signed on a new model for your agency," I retorted. "I gave him one of my business cards and made him promise to swing by with his composite and fill out our contract forms. The rest was all business, too, which I might remind you, came about because you suggested I get involved with Kevin's phone friend – Jaime!"

"Touché, my dear. And forget about the five hundred, I was just steamed at little at my bad luck in blackjack."

"Don't worry, I forgot it the minute you told me about taking it out of my salary. I haven't received any salary to take it out of."

"Don't end with a preposition. See you at the office tomorrow. I think Kevin and I will head straight home for a little R and R."

"That went well, I guess, except for the mysterious bags which disappeared before we could examine them," I mused aloud as the elevator whisked us up to our penthouse in the sky.

Andres just held me tighter, his body working against mine, his intent clearly noted. I quickly let us in to the apartment. He pulled me toward the bedroom. That's all for today!

He didn't show up the next day at the office. He showed up at the beach. Right below our ocean side balcony where I had first seen him. The body lay there in the cool of the morning, stretched out on the sand as if waiting for the first intense tanning rays of the day.

I could almost 'copy and paste' the descriptive scene from earlier in these pages, but for one detail – he was not laying on a stainless steel table in the morgue with an 'unknown white male' on his toe tag. He was known, he had a name, he was José. Death for one, but life remained for the rest of us. What more can I say…?

Chapter Six

Rafael was the first one I summoned to the hot seat. He had known more about José's trip than he'd let on. Andres took the day off from school to be here with me as I quizzed his friend about the tragedy.

Coffee on the terrace, a casual setting. Catch him candidly and off guard. Andres would be my buffer zone, to keep me from getting too tough with the Ice Man if he didn't tell all. I needed info on what we'd gotten into before it spilled over into our own lives. As if it hadn't already!

"What did you forget to tell us?" I began.

"Keep your doors locked!" he warned.

"Thanks! And your friend José, did he get the same warning?"

After an hour of further enlightenment on the subject of José, Rafael took his leave. He wasn't going to classes today either – going home to lock his doors, so he said.

"Let's go into the office this morning," I suggested quietly to Andres. "This is way too much information for us to process alone. We need to let Bradley in on it anyway."

Within the next ten minutes, the nose of the sleek black Corvette slipped out into late morning traffic and headed north toward Lincoln Road. Andres was driving, I was riding shotgun.

The office of Model Solutions was eerily quiet on this weekday morning as we entered through the outer reception area and into the main conference room. Isabel wasn't due to take over until one o'clock. We summoned Bradley by phone from his magazine publishing office down the hallway. I put the coffee on. We'd need it.

"What's so earth shattering you couldn't give me a hint over the telephone," he queried as he breezed into the room.

"We just grilled Rafael," I began, with a sidelong glance at Andres remembering my use of that word once before. "I think it's going to be a bumpy ride for all of us if we continue poking our noses into this José business."

"I think it's a bit late to pull back now – he's dead. We have to do something about it," Bradley sputtered. "We just can't ignore the injustice of it all like we did with that gambling ship and the phony money when you and Andres helped me search for Kevin."

I drew a deep breath and stared!

"Counterfeit cash, a gambling ship, the sleazy go-to man from the bar on Espanola Way – they're all connected!" I exclaimed. "That's what this is about!"

"What did I miss?" Bradley piped up, a confused look clouding his face.

"José had two satchels full of cash from the Bahamas that he was transporting to Miami. That's got to be it."

"But why kill the carrier?" Andres ventured.

"Probably skimmed some of the money off the top, not knowing it was fake! Rafael said he had a lot of cash on him when he showed up at his door Sunday night. The proceeds from the skim?"

A dropped pin could have been heard hitting the plush carpet at that point.

"That could have gotten him killed if someone wanted to keep the fake money off the street until it was paid out to winners on a gambling boat," I observed.

"What do we do now?" My words echoed through the room.

I placed another call to Rafael. I needed him to contact Mr. Go-To for a face to face. He might be our only link between José and the destination for the two sacks of money.

He called me back – it was set for two o'clock at the dark smoky bar on Espanola Way. Andres and I would go alone so Bradley could get back to work.

"You don't mind waiting outside with Rafael while I meet with the sleaze? I don't want him to see who you are."

"I'll keep the Ice Man occupied for you," he grinned. "We'll be your backup if anything goes wrong."

"What could go wrong, we're in the middle of South Beach?"

Two o'clock straight up: Rafael and Andres lounging across the street and me strolling casually toward the entrance of El Morro Bar and Grill. I pushed through the swinging door into the bar area. Rancid odors of smoke and cooking grease hung in the air. The last table on the far wall was occupied by one scumbag character straight out of a 'Miami Vice' still shot. It was my contact man, Mr. Go-To.

"You know why I'm here?" I began.

He looked up disinterestedly through the bloodshot eyes of a man who's seen too much liquor and not enough fresh ocean breezes.

"You lookin' for more guys for your new club?" he said quietly. "Now I remember who you are from the last time you was in here."

"I'm looking for a particular guy, the one you set up on the photo shoot in Bimini."

"Don't know who you mean?"

"You called him the skinny blonde kid with no talent."

"Oh, that one. Yeah, I remember him."

"He's dead! They found him stretched out on the beach. An apparent overdose."

"Don't know nothin' 'bout that," he whined.

"The guys you sent him to, who were they?"

And so it went, on and on. Me accusing, him denying. I wasn't getting anywhere. One last shot to stir the pot.

"If they want their money back, they should call me."

"What money you talkin' 'bout?"

"Some of the counterfeit stuff that was about to hit the street. They'll know what I mean."

"How do I get a hold of ya?"

"Call the Ice Man, he'll let me know."

I turned and left the bar, wondering if I had just set myself up for big trouble. Time to gather the troops and wait.

"You did what?" Bradley exclaimed when we got back to the office. "You've just put your foot in it – and way too deep. You guys are staying with me for the next couple of days."

"He's right," I said, turning to Andres. "They must know where we live. José was left on our doorstep as a warning."

"Don't even go back for your clothes. You can buy new," he advised. "As of this moment we all change our patterns. No coming to the office, no going to classes, no strolling on the beach. We hunker down and stay in."

"Yes, mother," I grinned. "I love it when you get all bossy and take charge."

The plan was set in motion. Andres and I would return home, casually, and stash the car in our garage space. We'd take a quiet stroll down the beachside boardwalk, hand in hand. At South Pointe Park, Bradley would make a slow drive through the congestion, stop, we'd hop in the back seat, and then he'd drive across the causeway to downtown Miami. From there it would be cunning and luck, trying to spot a tail before returning via one of the other causeways to Miami Beach.

As we sat around Bradley's dining table enjoying a scrumptious but late lunch picked up along the way back at Epicure Market in South Beach, I began with, "I need to call 'Calvin the Cooler Guy'."

"Huh? The 'what' guy?"

"You remember, my buddy at the Miami-Dade County Morgue?"

"I forgot you used to be in the 'death care' business," Bradley groaned. "How gruesome."

"Death is a 'fact of life', after all."

"You just ruined my appetite!" Bradley exclaimed. "And you know how much I love kosher."

Calvin had a lot of info that I could share with the rest of the South Beach Boyz, but no conclusions were officially drawn. Cause of death in the records would read, 'pending further studies, manner of death unclassified'.

"That's it?" Bradley exhorted. "He's found dead on a public beach with needle marks in his veins and they can't figure out what killed him?"

"They have to be certain. Toxicological screenings, time of death, manner of ingestion, etc. That's usually the way it goes. We know it's murder, but they don't know s---!"

"Now what," Bradley fumed, "we just sit and wait for someone to come after us?"

"Calvin did give me the name of the investigating detective here in the Miami Beach Police Homicide Unit."

"Miami Beach *has* a homicide unit? Who knew?"

"They won't tell us anything, but if I take Jaime along, maybe they will tell him. He is the domestic partner, if they still have that sort of thing here in Miami Beach."

"They used to," Bradley confirmed. "Don't know how it is now. That sort of thing never interested me anyway. Love is in the heart, darlin', not on a piece of notarized paper."

"Amen!" I said, turning to Andres with a great big smile.

I called Jaime at his apartment, left a message on the machine. He was to meet me in front of 1100 Washington Avenue, in the morning at 9 AM.

The dawn was breaking out of the east, skies clear, and winds whipping around as I stood on one of the balconies of Bradley's penthouse condo, staring blankly toward the ocean. It had been an uneasy night. Tossing and turning, thinking and planning – to no avail. It would be what it would be, or so I've heard. I couldn't rewrite this story, just watch it unfold and throw my two cents worth into the pot.

After an early breakfast, Andres, Bradley, and me at the table, I set off the Miami Beach Police Department alone. I didn't want the other two involved any further than they already were. Jaime was waiting, smoking a cigarette, pacing nervously, as I approached the front of the building.

"I thought models didn't smoke," I commented.

He threw the butt to the ground, crushing it under the heel of his boot. No wonder he looked taller, I thought, noting the edge of the Tony Lamas sticking out from under the slightly flared jeans. Sexy, sexy, sexy! An uncontrolled shudder passed over me.

"Let's get this over with," he mumbled, "I don't like police stations."

Chapter Seven

The whole trip was a waste. They knew nothing, they offered no advice, no counseling, and no information. Jaime was bored, I was disappointed, and Detective Lt. Devereaux was tight lipped about the details of the investigation. No personal effects were found, no phony currency, not even a dime of cash.

"You were a big help!" I accused, as we walked out of the station together. "Don't you even care about what happened to your boyfriend?"

"What do you expect from me? He's gone, I gotta move on with my life."

"You have no idea why he was in Bimini, or why he was smuggling cash into the States. Or where he might have stashed his 'cut'?" I pressed.

He stared blankly at me, turned and walked away.

"They'll be after you next," I called out as he rounded the corner.

"That went well!" I vented sarcastically as I entered PH 12 through the unlocked front door. "I thought you were keeping things secure around here!"

"I just got back with my four grocery bags and didn't have enough hands," Bradley puffed. "What's got you in such a state?"

"Where's Andres?" I queried, more calmly.

"At the pool, looking forlorn and frustrated. He wants to go back to classes."

"Yeah, we'd all like to go back to our normal lives," I admitted. A pause ensued as this thought triggered the outline of a plan in my mind, so I blurted out my initial thoughts, "That's exactly what we should do. Go back to 'situation normal' and draw them out, whoever *they* are."

"You know that old acronym – S.N.A.F.U." Bradley warned. "We don't want to make things worse!"

"It could be entirely coincidental that José's body ended up behind our building," I speculated. "He was last seen alive in Rafael's condo which is somewhere in our South Beach neighborhood."

"You still don't have an address for that guy? What kind of a detective are you?"

"He's a very private person, especially south of Fifth Street, and very protective of his life there. I think he lives with some older guy who's paying all the bills and travels a lot."

"I think I know more that one of those types," Bradley observed.

"Don't be throwing any stones my way," I defended. "You and your blonde bimbo are no different."

"Touché!"

The door burst open and Andres entered, stifling any further comments.

"Hey, champ!" I greeted. "We were just talking about you."

Andres drew me into his arms and whispered, "I really need to go back to school, baby. I don't want to get left behind."

"I'll get lunch ready while you two iron out the details," Bradley said diplomatically as he fled to the kitchen.

Andres really knows how to work me. I'm putty in his hands, but he was right of course, so we agreed to a compromise. I would drive him to school and pick him up after classes. No more standing at the bus stop, and I would go back to my routine – working mornings in the modeling agency and afternoons at my writing.

"Luncheon is served on the terrace," Bradley announced archly. "Chili dogs with genuine Skyline Chili from Cincinnati. And Graeters Ice Cream for dessert – also made in Cincinnati. That should soothe the beast in your soul!"

"Doesn't sound very kosher to me," I exclaimed, "but I do appreciate the 'nod' to my hometown, Cincinnati."

"Publix sells everything these days," Bradley confirmed. "Besides, who cares about kosher anyway? I'm not cut and neither are you."

"What is 'cut" mean, Rick?" Andres questioned with wide-eyed innocence.

My face turned slightly pink as I deferred the answer with, "I'll explain it all later."

Bradley just chuckled, the twinkle in his eye let me know it was all a big ice breaker, as he added, "We've all been just a little too serious around here lately, 'dontcha think, Blanche'?"

And so the day passed into night, the night into day, and so on, and so on.

We were getting back to our lives all right, but no further into our mystery of 'the body on the beach', or how José ended up dead on the sandy edge of the boardwalk outside the base of our condo building.

Bradley and I had begun our usual breakfast meetings, over coffee and Danish, with one slight change. We no longer whiled away the hours at News Café, but took our 'working' meetings in the office of Model Solutions. I could still answer the phones, and Bradley was just steps away from his publishing office down the hall.

"No news from your informants?" Bradley queried, as he idly picked the raisins from the iced cinnamon roll at hand.

"Nothing is happening. Andres is back at school, Rafael riding with him in the 'vette. I'm back to the bus routine. Situation normal."

"I think you need to stir the pot a little."

"How do you mean?" I asked with puzzled frown.

"Follow the money. For starters, find out from your police detective if any counterfeit cash has turned up recently in the 'beach' neighborhood."

"Oh yeah! Like I should march into police headquarters and say I know José was 'muling' phony currency from the Bahamas, but I didn't think it necessary to report it!"

"Just how *did* you know, Bradley asked, "that it was counterfeit, I mean?"

"Well, I…"

I looked away for a second, jumbled thoughts churning through my mind.

"Rafael had told me to watch out for José on his cruise…but he never said why exactly," I said slowly. "I just assumed when he brought those big duffel bags in from the boat, they were full of cash or drugs."

"But you didn't know *what* you were looking for?"

"Not really," I muttered. "I just figured it was money – being such big canvas totes and all."

"Then what gave you the idea it was counterfeit cash?" he pushed on."

"When you brought up the gambling ship and Kevin, I guess…"

"So no one has actually ever confirmed what was in those bags?"

"Not really…I assumed…'

"I rest my case!" Bradley announced, rising from his chair to refill our coffee mugs. "You don't know, you assumed!"

"I've an idea," I exclaimed. "You know those old movie mysteries where the detective invites all his suspects to one place for a gathering like a dinner or a party?"

"Like the old 'Thin Man' flicks from the 1930's?" Bradley replied.

"Only updated – a cocktail party with a lot of innocents for window dressing and all the 'usual suspects' for the real targets of the game."

"So you want to have a cocktail party? Invite Rafael, Jaime, and whomever, to your place for drinks and see what shakes out – while under the influence?"

"Not exactly. More like, you invite all your magazine advertisers, your photographers, publicity people. I invite all the models registered here at Model Solutions, we move casually through the melee and keep our eyes and ears on our targets."

"Sounds like much more than your little condo can handle," Bradley observed.

"But just about the perfect size for your four-bedroom penthouse in the sky," I grinned slyly as I continued, "with all those terraces and splendid views of the city, with the ocean on one side and Biscayne Bay on the other."

"And just who is paying for all this?" Bradley huffed.

"It's all tax deductible; you own the publishing company, the magazine, and the modeling agency. Let the accountant sort it out."

"I've got to get back to work," Bradley announced, getting up from his seat in my office. "Most expensive breakfast meeting I've ever had," he muttered as he slipped out the door.

And the invitations went out to all Bradley's contacts from his infamous rolodex, known to contain contact information for every modeling agent, photographer, coach, product placement artist, talent scout, and production agent known to exist in South Florida. I was put in charge of contacting every model in our database at Model Solutions, with instructions to dress 'fit to kill' in their finest and most fabulous wardrobe selections. This was not a test, it was the real thing. We were seeking jobs for every one of them as well as a little private detecting on the side, by yours truly.

Two weeks hence:

(In other words, it took a couple of weeks to get the ball rolling, I didn't know it was going to be *this* big a production, or I might have backed off my suggestion...)

"Who designed those invitations, anyway?" I asked Bradley as we stood in the entrance hall looking at the frantic activity around us.

"My staff can be very creative when they have to be."

"But no address, no time and date, no details...?"

"That's the creative part, it insures the purity of our guest list."

"The purity...?"

"When they call for details, we get our guest list and keep an air of exclusivity and mystery. Keeps the gangsters and riff-raff out, too."

"Ah, I see."

YOU ARE CORDIALLY INVITED TO

MODEL SOLUTIONS

RUNWAY PARTY

AT THE PENTHOUSE OF BRADLEY PUBLICATIONS

R.S.V.P. SOUTHERN EXPOSURE MAGAZINE

MIAMI BEACH, FLORIDA

Chapter Eight

Bradley once again, I have to admit, had everything under control. The event at his penthouse on Saturday evening had been a smashing success. 'Monday-morning quarterbacking' took place in the Model Solutions office over coffee and Danish as usual:

"Well, my dear, did you get anything useful out of your suspects?"

"Still don't know 'who dunnit' but both Rafael and Jaime had more than enough motive, and both are still in my gun sights."

"Tell me more."

"Let's start with the unknowns, the mob, or whatever they really are. They could be out there just waiting for a chance to get one of us, but if we continue to blame everything on them, we're not going to get anywhere with this investigation."

"Because…?"

"They will never be found, never accused, and never brought to justice." I paused to let that sink in before adding, "They are much too clever to kill José, place his lifeless body under our balcony, draw the attention of the police, and still not have their phony money back. Even if there is counterfeit money floating around, they're not going to link themselves to it in this very public way. These are not the days of Tony Montana and the cocaine cowboys of the movie 'Scarface'. "

"I suppose that makes sense. The whole premise of the money is totally unconfirmed."

"Au contraire, the money *is* real; it's the counterfeit part we'll never establish."

"And you know about the money…how?"

"Rafael let slip to Andres during the height of your party, that José had given him an envelope with several thousand dollars in it to hold for him, the day before he was found dead."

"Only a couple of thousand? That's no motive for murder."

"Exactly!" I agreed. "Which brings us to suspect number two – Jaime."

"Do tell, but let me fill up our cups. I think better with caffeine floating through my system."

"That's what I've always said, coffee and chocolate…"

I took my notes in hand for close scrutiny while Bradley replenished our brain food in the reception office. I've learned to carry my notebook around with me at all times and write down immediately anything pertinent while the info is fresh. Memory is a fickle friend at best – and much too selective.

"Ah, the famous notebook…anything in there about me – throw it out immediately!"

"You'd plead the fifth anyway."

"Please go on with 'door number two'."

"Yes, your Kevin is much cleverer than I suspected. He wangled things out of Jaime I'd never even thought of asking."

"Such as…?"

"The boots the other day at the police station were just the tip of the iceberg."

"What boots are you talking about?"

"The new Tony Lamas he wore in my presence."

"You would notice something like that. You've got a fetish for leather boots, tight jeans, and slender young men, if I recall from your previous memoirs."

"I do write fiction – remember?"

"Get back to clever Kevin please. He needs all the praise he can get."

"Jaime has spent an enormous amount on fashionable new clothes recently, according to Kevin. It turns out he came in to a substantial amount of money."

"Jaime actually confided all this to my Kevin?"

"No. Turns out Kevin had the 'wisdom' to casually question some of the other models that had gone on the last photo shoot with the two of them. They confirmed the story. He's been seen at several high end stores on Lincoln Road – and carrying clothing bags with their costly merchandise logoed all over the outside."

"So much for the usual jeans and tee I've seen him in..." Bradley mused.

"Exactly. Where did *that* money come from at this particular time?"

We left the question dangle in the air as we both returned to our usual Monday morning duties. Bradley retired to his office with a quiet thoughtful air about him. I typed up my inner most thoughts while they were still fresh. The computer helps me keep an organized file on everyone and includes both fact and conjecture. And you wondered where all this stuff comes from that appears in my books?

The revelations for the day were not quite over yet:

A silent and empty apartment welcomed me with open arms as I slipped through the doorway with bags of groceries and sundry supplies. Luckily we had a small food market on Collins Avenue at Sixth Street, just close enough to my bus stop for picking up a few necessaries on the walk home.

I was starting lunch prep when the love of my life burst through the front door.

"Guess who's coming to dinner?"

"I can't imagine! We're having dinner?'

"Not now, I see you fixing a lunch for just the two of us. This is for later."

Did I detect a mischievous gleam in his eye?

"I'm listening," I said apprehensively.

"Your very favorite mystery man."

"Uh-oh, the Ice Man cometh!"

"You got it. I'll cook and you question."

"What brought this on all of sudden?"

"He invited himself. Said he needed to see you as soon as possible, so I said, 'Let's make it dinner'."

"Well, that is very…mysterious…" Loss of words accompanied the turning wheels inside my head and the dazed countenance of my face.

"Rick, you okay?"

"Ah, yes, just very…surprised."

I'll skip the dinner menu of that evening, and the 'across the table' chatter between the two students in my presence, and get right to the important stuff. At least, important as it pertains to this José business.

We had moved out onto the terrace to enjoy the incoming breezes off the ocean, an unknown luxury in my past residences. Andres was cleaning up in the kitchen, I had poured drinks and brought them out with me on a tray, and Rafael was staring intently – at me!

"I'm going to entrust this to you – you're the older and wiser one around here." He slipped an envelope into my hand before continuing, "This is the money José asked me to hold for him. I don't know what to do with it now that he's not around."

He turned away quickly so I couldn't see his eyes. But I knew what was going on, the tears were forming. He was too macho to let me in on the tender side of his feelings, but he had them just the same.

"Do you know how much it is?" I asked quietly.

"No, I never looked, it was sealed."

And so it was, still sealed.

"I'll have my employer lock it up in his company safe, if that's all right with you. We can't keep it here. If any family shows up to claim him, we'll turn it over to them."

"Don't let Jamie know you got it."

"No way."

And so that was the last that was said about José, money, mystery, or intrigue. The guys talked about school, I only listened with half and ear as my thoughts were elsewhere.

"What did he need to see you for?" Andres asked after Rafael had gone home.

"José's legacy. He had left some money with Rafael, which he just turned over to me."

"What is it? That funny money you were worried about?"

"I'm not sure. I think we should just have Bradley lock it up for safekeeping until we get this thing sorted out."

It was late, a school night as well. We left everything as is and called it a day.

"Bradley, I think we can rule out Rafael."

"Ah, suspect number one had an alibi?"

"No, but a lot of emotion. He really cared about José. I don't think he had anything to do with it."

He pursued the raisins again. Plucking them out of the Danish.

"Why do you order them, if you don't eat them?"

"Eat what?"

"The friggin' raisins!"

"I do, eventually. It just helps me to think."

I'm leaving that alone – raisin logic?

"Rafael entrusted an envelope of money to me. It's José's stash. Will you keep it in your company safe until family shows up?"

"If we had one."

"Can you lock it up somewhere?"

"I'll take care of it. How much is there?"

"I don't think we should open it."

"Afraid what you'll find? Like the counterfeit cash?"

"No, I'm beginning to think we got something wrong here. The pieces just aren't falling into place yet."

"I'll leave you to it, got work of my own to do. Why don't you give that Jaime guy a call, check up on his sudden display of wealth?"

"Good idea. I'll just come out and ask him – where'd you get all that money?" I was being sarcastic again, I'm actually quite good at it.

"That's the idea. We have to quit tiptoeing around this thing or it will never make any sense."

Bradley and envelope left the office. I pondered in silence.

"Well, why not?" I said aloud, to an empty room. "Can't hurt to just ask."

Jaime agreed to stop by the office the next day. He was tied up on a job right now. What job? He didn't get it through our agency. Hmm. Man overboard...?

Noon the next day, never in the morning. What is it with these models, do they sleep away until lunch time?

He came through the door, boots and all. Clothing was a cut above the usual, but nothing outlandishly screaming Armani. A & F or Hollister, at best. I do love to see a hot guy in Abercrombie jeans, however, it brings a shiver to my soul, as well as other parts better left unmentioned here. This book is a level above my previous tales.

"You're looking fashionable today," I greeted, just to cut to the point. "I hear you've upgraded your wardrobe. A photo shoot going down that we don't know about?"

Putting him on the immediate defensive was my new tactic.

"Got to talk to you about that. I'm signing with another agency. They're taking me to New York."

Talk about a splash of cold water...

"I know you been askin' around about me. I got nothin' to hide. The new guys fronted me some cash to get my stuff updated before I leave town."

"Leave town? So much for your loyalty to José."

"Yeah, about José…there's some things you don't know."

"Like the fights between you two, his cuts and bruises, his sudden disappearances. I know more than you think."

"You don't the real story here."

"Well, tell me. You asked me to help you find him, and then you beat him up when you got him back. Some relationship you guys had!"

"Will you just listen to me…?" he insisted.

"Sorry, now go ahead."

"José's been messed up with heroin ever since we met. I just didn't know about it at first. He got to smashin' his fist into the wall, breakin' a glass out o' the window, passin' out on the floor. That's where all that bruisin' come from."

I remained stoic and silent while he was on a roll.

"You wouldn't know about that stuff from where you come from."

He just didn't know how *much* I knew about 'that stuff'. Marco and me in Key West. We went through the same rough times 'til he got caught and put in jail. (Read 'Key West Connections' for the whole story)

"I had about as much as any guy could take. I loved him as best I could, but it didn't make him change his ways." He paused and looked away – that lost in space look, before continuing, "The last time he went out on a shoot to Bimini, he came back with some money and a whole lot of…the stuff. I told him he had to leave, he couldn't live with me no more 'til he straightened his life around."

The stillness ensued. Jaime had his fresh memories of a drug addict at the bottom. I had my own, from the distant past.

"I never saw him again. Until that day."

"What day?" I snapped back to the present.

"They had me go look at him in the morgue place." He brushed something away from his eyes. "They took his stuff from the apartment to look over for evidence. Asked me a lot of questions."

I kept my secret, the evident flight to Rafael's place, the envelope. What difference could that make to Jaime now? He had enough to think about already.

"So you're really leaving us?" I ventured.

"Got to start fresh, somewhere else, forget about Miami Beach. It'll eat you right up."

Yeah, just wait until he gets to New York, I thought. Different scene, but same problems.

"What about his family? You know them?"

"He only mentioned a sister, up in Kissimmee or Orlando somewhere. Police said they'd get the phone number out of his things and let them know what happened. I don't want to be here when they come down. They don't need to know the things I know about him."

The rest of the conversation was very general. I wished him well in New York. He was no longer a suspect in my book. Two down, none to go. Right back where we started from.

Luckily for me, Isabel came in at that moment to take over. I had too much on my mind to work or write. Time for a fresh scene.

I opted for a walk home as the best remedy. Clears your head as you dodge past tourists, skateboarders, and side walk tables lining Ocean Drive. I forgot how hot it would be, dressed in my corporate casual and toting my laptop in its carrying case.

Where to go next, I thought, trudging through the sand. I was skirting around through the park next to our condo building for another look at the crime scene, amend that to 'place where the body was found'. We had no proof yet of anything.

Nothing had changed except the sand, raked smooth, as customary on a public beach in South Florida. No visions popped into my brain, no ideas. I went in through the gated back pool deck and into the elevator lobby.

My cell rang as I rode up to the top floor. The number looked familiar, sort-of, so I answered.

"Hey Rick, Calvin here."

"Calvin, how'd you get my number?"

"You called me at work the other day, remember? I save all incoming caller ID's. Never know when you're going to need the contact info in this business."

"Yeah, I forgot how detail oriented you are. What you got for me?"

"The tox screen came back on your buddy."

"Not really a buddy, just working the case for his roommate."

"Bottom line, heroin overdose."

"That matches up with his history."

"The odd thing about it, all the needle marks and scars on his arms were old. They found the fresh track between his toes."

"What's the significance of that?"

"Whether self-injected or he had help, it was designed to conceal the cause of death."

"Doesn't make any sense," I pondered aloud.

"The cause of death is now official; the 'manner of death' still reads 'pending further investigation'."

"He still there?"

"Nah, they come down from Kissimmee last night and took him back for the funeral."

I reached my floor, stepped out of the elevator, and dropped the phone.

"Calvin, you still there?" I grabbed the phone quickly from the marble paved hallway.

"Yeah, what happened, you got spooked?"

"No, juggling too much in my hands trying to get in my door."

"S'alright, man!" He paused, then added, "You take care now, Rick, got to get back to work."

"Thanks, Calvin. I really appreciate your help." Not unexpected, the heroin part, but 'between the toes'? What was the purpose?

Chapter Nine

A mystery within a mystery. Don't you just love it? The multi-layered world of crime in real life mimicking computer games! I reported these lab results to Bradley over the conference table next morning.

"Since Jose's family has claimed his remains, what do we do about the money?" I asked.

"Let's think about *how* we do it, not what we do," he suggested.

"Good point."

We tabled that discussion for later, as there was other business at hand.

"And the manner of injection?" I prompted. "It leads me to no conclusion."

And we tabled this one, too.

Bradley had his work, I had my work. The José story would be continued later.

And a full week went by before we brought it up at our breakfast conference again.

"About that envelope," Bradley began.

"What envelope?"

"The money!"

"Oh, yes, what do we do with it?" I pondered aloud.

"Easiest thing is to Fed Ex it to his family," Bradley suggested.

"The right thing to do, but I hate to think about it getting lost in some Miami Beach Police Property Room, is to turn it over to Detective, ah, hmm…Devereaux. How could I forget that name? Straight out of a New Orleans crime movie."

"And tell him what – it's been sitting in our office for weeks?"

"Got a point there," I admitted.

"Should we open it first and see how much money we're dealing with here?"

"Then we're responsible for what's inside. You want that responsibility?"

And then there was silence…guilty silence?

"Go ahead and open it. We'll see how much, and then decide what to do," I urged.

"I did already. There's five thousand dollars and a short note."

"You what!?! Now you tell me!" I exploded.

"Calm down, I just had to know how much we were responsible for, the amount of money, that is!"

The pregnant pause ensued. (I've used that expression before and just love it!)

"What's in the note?" I pressed.

"You're not going to like it…"

He fiddled in his coat pocket, and then pushed the folded sheet of paper to me. I unfolded and read in silence.

"Oh, that's just dandy, now we *have* to turn it in to the police."

"Looks like a suicide note to me," Bradley said smugly. "Case closed."

"Not necessarily," I ventured, "something's not right here."

"Such as?"

"It doesn't look like his handwriting."

"How do you know what his hand-*printing* looks like, anyway?"

"We have a note he left the morning he fled from our house in the wee hours."

"Leave it to you to f--- up a good solid ending to this case," Bradley huffed.

"Such language from my editor!" I teased. "You keep the money and the note in your – whatever space you kept it in. Tomorrow I'll bring Jose's real hand-printed note in. We'll do the comparison, go on from there."

And we did, the next day, compare the notes side by side on the conference table, Danish and coffee cups pushed safely out of the way.

"See this handwritten note found on our dining table the morning he left? The printing is sloppy, mis-spelled words – a mess!"

"You said he'd been acting spacey anyway, could be a druggie's attempt at a quick note."

"Look at this carefully worded, correctly spelled, neatly written specimen you took from the envelope."

"I see your point," Bradley conceded. "But who else could have written it?"

"It came from Rafael, to me, and to you," I paused, "and the chain of evidence is unbroken, but…"

"Go on," Bradley urged, "you're on a roll."

"Now there are three confirmed sets of fingerprints on the note and envelope. If José wrote this, there will be four sets, at the very least."

"Who's going to test for prints, Mr. Detective?"

"The police will have to take over now, I can't do it."

The pause again, we get a lot of those as our two sets of wheels are churning though this mess.

"And we're going to need samples from you, me, Andres, and Rafael, for the process of elimination. That's the tough part!"

"I can just see the four of us charging into Lt. Whatever's office and trying to explain this whole bungled mess!" Bradley fumed.

"You opened the envelope!" I let that thought sit for processing.

"Let's get back to this later," Bradley advised, "I've got pressing work to do and you have, too."

He left the office with the money, the pair of notes, and did go back to work, but I had a plan and had to think it through first. It involved bringing Raphael into Model Solutions for a conference.

I broached the subject of Rafael with Andres while we were dining al fresco - out on the terrace, in case your Italian is no better than mine.

"Think Rafael and you could come in Saturday morning, to the office I mean?"

"Sure, no classes. What's up?"

"Bradley opened the envelope."

"It's bad, huh?'

"Just unexpected. I want to watch his body language again."

"You mean you want *me* to watch it like before," he grinned.

"I'll go in early, tidy up a few details, and you bring Rafael along about eleven or so."

"Setting the stage – right?"

"You catch on fast, no wonder your grades are so good."

Cut to Saturday:

"Bradley, we need Danish and coffee. This has got to look casual, not like a police interrogation room!"

"Already done. You didn't look in the conference room!"

"Oh, sorry."

"I'll go back to my office down the hall, you call when they get here. It'll look better that way – real casual."

"Yeah, got a few things to finish up in here anyway."

He left the office, I got down to the task at hand – rigging up a recorder.

Andres and Rafael ambled in at eleven o'clock, precisely.

"So this is where the magic happens," Andres noted, as he glanced around the office, taking particular note of the showcased photos on the walls. "No wonder you love your work," he grinned, "all these hot guys coming in to see you."

I was saved from answering by the immediate arrival of Bradley. Probably had his door open down the hallway just waiting for their appearance.

"Don't worry about Rick and those models," Bradley assured him, "your honey does the paperwork, and I meet with *all* clientele."

He stared at Rafael intently as if noticing him for the very first time, before adding, "We don't have your photos on file, do we?"

"That's not my thing," he mumbled in return, face turning slightly pink with embarrassment.

"Well, if you change your mind…," Bradley let the thought dangle as he entered the conference room ahead of us.

I knew what he was up to, throwing Rafael slightly off balance and into a defensive mode.

"Everyone, help yourself to the Danish and coffee," he offered, with a dramatic gesture as he directed us to seats around the conference table, in the positions we had preplanned. "We've got sad news for everyone here!"

We all looked up expectantly as his voice had turned very somber.

"The envelope in my safekeeping these past few weeks has to be passed along to Jose's family," he stated while pausing for dramatic effect – leave it to Bradley, our resident drama queen!

He fished into the large manila folder he had carried into the room with him. It was the large expanding type, the kind you might store folders and documents in. He pulled out three large plastic zip lock bags, and scooted one over in front of each of us.

"Now then, pick up the item in front of you," he directed, "and tell me in essence what you see."

Clever, Bradley, very clever, I thought to myself, you're collecting a set of fingerprints from each of us.

"Andres," he began, "what do you see in the bag? Check out both sides, and describe it."

"A plain envelope, nothing on the front, nothing on the back. Someone's slit it open across the top," he offered, bewilderment all over his face.

"Yes, very good," Bradley said. "I opened it to count the money before I put it in the safe."

"You said you didn't have a safe," I chimed in.

The dark looks came my way before he answered, "I was speaking metaphorically!"

"How do you spell that?" I kidded, pretending to jot down notes like a reporter.

"Now, Rick, when you're done being clever, tell me what's in your bag?"

"Three thousand dollars, cash, all hundreds."

"And you can see the amount clearly through the bag without opening it?" he questioned.

"You know I counted it before, when you opened the envelope," I insisted. "It's all fanned out now and I see thirty one hundred dollar bills, all crisp and new looking."

"Okay, and now Rafael, tell me what you see through the plastic. Check out both sides."

"A note on plain white paper."

"What's the note say?" he pushed on.

Rafael looked crestfallen, sad, anything but surprised. I wonder why?

He read the note aloud:

Sorry Sis, I just can't take it anymore.
Please use this money for your kids.
I don't want them turning out like me.
I love all of you,   Jose

We sat in stunned silence, well, some of us *looked* stunned. Mostly Andres, but Rafael appeared less surprised. Not a very good actor?

I glanced at Bradley, but he motioned me to silence with a slight hand gesture. He was waiting for a *verbal* reaction. He didn't get it.

"I'm going to pass around notepads to each of you," he began, as he removed a stack of them from the credenza behind his chair at the head of the table, if a round table can have a head! "You're each to write down exactly what you have observed inside your packet. No editorializing, no guess work. Just describe exactly what you see."

Aha! Now he's going to analyze handwriting – Rafael's in particular.

In ten minutes, pencils down, just like test taking at school, Bradley passed around the accordion file for each of us to deposit his packet, notepad and pencil inside for safekeeping. He pulled the elastic strap up around, and placed it back on the credenza behind him.

"More coffee, anyone?" he offered.

The boys had gone. Bradley and I were each deep in thought, sharing the same space – my office, but in two different worlds.

"He's very clever," Bradley observed aloud.

"And very guilty," I offered. "The cool act just doesn't cover it."

"Now what?" he pondered aloud.

"We'll take it to Detective Devereaux Monday morning."

"We?"

"Of course - we. You and I are both witnesses to what went down here this morning, and I have the tape recording to verify it."

"Why do I have to go?"

"You're the clever one that came up with this fingerprint and hand writing idea. I was just going for the tape recording."

Silence! But I broke it with a little buttering up.

"I didn't know you had all that cleverness in you," I began.

"You thought that just because I look like a dizzy blonde and sometimes act like Nathan Lane, that I don't have a brain? How do you think a poor country boy like me got to be a prominent business man in Miami Beach?"

"The way you tell it, your plantation days in the good old south didn't prepare you for anything but dressing like a dandy and sipping mint juleps."

"We farmed – in the field! Plowin', plantin', and pickin'!"

"Was that in Alabama or Georgia?" I kidded.

"Both. The house was in Georgia, the Upper Hundred in Alabama."

"The upper hundred?"

"The plantin' fields were northwest of the main house and the state line ran right through the place. We literally 'crossed the line' to get to work each day."

"Sorry I asked!"

"Google it next time you get on that computer of yours. It's on Providence-Church Road. I assume you are getting your book in order? I want the unedited proof on my desk by next week."

"But my story is not finished yet. We still need to solve this case."

"I need to see what you've got written to make sure we're going to make our printing deadline."

"Now we have a printing deadline?"

"I've worked out a special rate with a new book publisher. It'll save us a bundle, but we have to have it 'in house' to them before the holidays to get that rate."

"Now you tell me. Nothing like putting on the pressure!"

"I'll go with you Monday morning just to make sure we get this situation with José resolved and move on 'with your book' and 'our modeling business'."

"An outstanding local business man like you standing alongside me, a poor peddler of prose, will add greatly to our credibility!"

Chapter Ten

And so it came to pass, Bradley and I quietly waited on a hard wooden bench outside the office of Homicide Detective Devereaux of the Miami Beach Police Department, waiting for our 'interview'.

An hour later, as we walked back toward Lincoln Road and the office:

"I could use a coffee in the fresh air and ambiance of Lincoln Road, surrounded by swirling masses of normal people who don't know what the inside of a police station looks like – at interrogation time."

"I'll buy, you pick the place," Bradley offered.

We ended up at Starbucks – where else? The time of the independent coffee houses like (fill in your favorite from the past – we all have one) are long since gone, victims of rising rents and name brand take-overs.

"Back in the day," I began, as we sipped caffeine at a sidewalk table, "this was a lot more fun, especially at night, with all the artsy people waiting in line for homemade pastries to go with their coffees, scrutinizing the wall art for sale, cruising the crowd. Now they just hover over their laptops and take up space. They've lost the art of cruising and conversation!"

Bradley stared moodily into space – a victim of police 'grilling'.

"I don't think they believed us," he finally said. "I'm afraid they're going to send the money along to his family and just close the file."

"Doesn't mean we have to quit," I interjected. "A mystery is *still* 'afoot', to misquote the master sleuth."

"You come up with something, and I'll back you. Meantime write the ending you assume will be the final truth. Then we can get *our* case closed. The book case!" he grinned at his own cleverness.

I rest *my* case...!

Since the morning at the police station and the coffee break at Lincoln Road ate up most of my work day, I headed directly home, after promising Bradley I would get right to work on my manuscript. Andres was already there, with Rafael, as I slipped through the door.

"Aha!" I was almost speechless with surprise, it does happens once in while.

"Rafael needs to talk to you about Saturday," Andres interjected before I could stammer out anything else.

"Rick, it's about the money," Rafael cut right in. "Supposed to be five thousand dollars not three thousand!"

"Aha!" again...? But he was correct, it was only three and I had seen the five when Bradley first showed me the contents. Hmm. Perhaps Bradley had set an additional trap for Rafael and forgot to tell me. I played along. "Thought he gave you a sealed envelope?"

Rafael's head dropped, as well as eyes, down and to the left. Was that the international sign of falsification? I think so.

"He must have told me how much when he asked me to hold it for him."

Neat save, but not convincing, so I pushed on, "And no mention of any note he was leaving in the package?"

"Nah, didn't say nothing but 'Hold this for me, I don't want Jamie to know I got money'."

"You just took his word for it? You didn't count it out?"

"Yeah, like I said, he trusted me and I trusted him." The pause, then, "He was a good kid, I cared about him. Sorry this happened to him."

"Yep, everyone's sorry but nobody did anything to help him. Now it's too late."

I stepped out onto the terrace to gaze at the water, sooth the mind, and think.

It helped. I knew who did it. I knew how they did it. I knew where they did it. Now to prove it!

I stepped back into the living room, Rafael had gone and Andres was making rattling noises in the kitchen.

"Your friend leave so soon?" I asked quietly.

"He thought you were angry with him," Andres replied turning to me with a strained expression.

"Guess I was a little harsh," I admitted, "but he's got something more to do with Jose's death than just holding the money."

"He really cared about him, he wouldn't hurt him in anyway."

"Could be it was someone else that administered that fatal drug overdose. I'm just saying, he knows something more than he's told us."

We turned to dinner preparations. Andres slightly aloof. Me wondering about Andres and *his* true relationship with Rafael?

Bradley - my mother confessor, my mentor, my consigliere, - in the office Tuesday morning, coffee, Danish, and notebooks spread all over the conference table. He looked up as I entered.

"What got under your tail this morning?" he began, with a smirk.

"Andres! You think he might be having an affair with Rafael?" I stammered out.

The look on his face, staring out at me through those round red-framed glasses, looking like Andy Warhol dressed as Sally Jessie Raphael, was priceless! On another cheerier day, I might actually have laughed out loud, but not today.

"Sex getting stale?"

"More like non-existent!"

"Ooh, that is bad, like me and what's his name, a few months ago."

"Kevin. Your boyfriend's name is Kevin!"

"Just trying to interject a little lightness and humor here," he joked. "I'm sure whatever's eating at Andres can be fixed if you'd just learn to communicate more and take him into your confidence."

I sat across the table and reached for my coffee which he had thoughtfully poured while he was expounding on my personal life.

"I thought I was."

"A little wine with dinner, roses on the table, chocolate something for dessert, after dinner drinks on the terrace... you get my drift. Then a quiet talk – pillow talk preferred, but if not possible at the moment make do with the sofa. You beside him and not across the table or the room."

I stared moodily out the doorway, not exactly hearing every word but getting the 'drift' as he said.

"You ask what's bothering him, then be a listener for a change."

"I thought I was." Again.

"You're so wrapped up in your case you forget that all this is new to Andres. He doesn't know the 'master sleuth' like I do. Give him patience and time and do the listening."

"Thanks, mom," I grinned, "just what I needed, a pep talk."

He turned to his paperwork, but not for long.

"I know who did it!"

"Did what?"

"Murdered José!"

Pin drop time. He squiggled around in his chair and looked out into the reception room before asking in a stage whisper, "Well, spill it!"

"The Go-To man, or Rafael, or the mysterious owner of the condo and benefactor of Rafael. They were all connected and they silenced José because he was the 'man who knew too much'!"

"No wonder Andres is holding out on you. You've just accused his best friend of complicity to the crime."

"Or his secret lover," I barely whispered it.

"Whose secret lover, Rafael's or Andres'?"

"Maybe they are one and the same."

"Don't even think it. You should be ashamed."

"I know. Speaking of being ashamed, who switched the money? That's what brought all this on in the first place."

"Oh, that! Just a ploy to draw out the killer maybe. If Rafael had anything to do with it then he would know the money count was incorrect."

"He did notice and came into our house and questioned me about it. Said he knew there was five thousand and not three thousand."

"I rest my case. Rafael did it."

"Now I'm not so sure," I admitted. "He would have kept quiet so as not to draw suspicion to himself in the first place."

"Point well taken," Bradley agreed. "Now what do we do?"

"After I leave work here today, I will make an appointment to see sleazy, greasy, Mr. Go-To and wring the truth out of him."

"Then I think you'd better have a back up man and a back up plan," he grimaced. "These guys play for keeps."

I elected to table that move until another day. I needed Andres on my side first, then he could be my backup, as he usually does. That's what lover's are for, isn't it?

By the time I got home, my mood had lifted. I was bearing packages of surprises for me to share with Andres. I had amends to make and I would even grovel if it would help win his approval and forgiveness. After all, I love him.

When at last I heard the front door open, the dinner preparations had been started, the table set – with roses, light orchid in color, I think the sales girl called them Sterling or something like that. The wine was chilled, a light rose', a white chocolate mousse had been purchased, I'm not tackling that kind of precision cooking, and a special surprise was waiting in the bedroom. Tell you later...

"Andres," I chimed out, "I'm so sorry about yesterday."

"What about yesterday?" he queried, looking perplexed.

"You were pissed off at me, and you had every right to be."

"I was upset with Rafael for following me into our home uninvited instead of going on down the block to his place as usual. I knew you wouldn't like anyone intruding on your privacy, Rick. I know you and I love you. I'd never be angry with you without talking it out first. You taught me that much."

"Oh dear, I've made a big mistake!"

"Well, if it means getting me roses and cooking dinner," he had evidently seen my setups already, "I'll try to do it more often."

"Do what?"

"Keep you slightly off-balance," he grinned. "I love gifts, but I love you more."

He put his arms around me and pulled me toward the bedroom.

"Can we postpone dinner for a few minutes?" he whispered into my ear.

And we did – postpone dinner – at least a couple of hours. Don't hear me complaining do you. After all, my life is all about Andres.

Chapter Eleven

"Looking positively ecstatic this morning like you've just been..."

"I am, and yes I was!" I gloated. "Situation 'normal' all..."

(We do edit the 'f' words when necessary!) (even the 'f')

Bradley was already hard at work in the conference room when I got in to the office, like a good boss should be.

"All is forgiven then?" he asked.

"Just a misunderstanding on my part. He was miffed at Rafael, not me. And he let me in on Rafael's big secret," I gloated.

"Do tell, I live for SoBe gossip."

"Rafael is not only *gay* he was Jose's secret lover!"

"Ooh, I didn't see that coming!"

"Neither did I. Mr Super-straight 'Ice Man' is just like the rest of us."

"I wouldn't go that far..."

"Sexually speaking, that is."

"So he didn't make a play for Andres?"

"Not likely. Andres said Rafael was so broken up about what happened to José, that he had to share his secret with someone he could trust - my Andres, the official secret keeper in our family."

"And you managed to get that little secret out of him with your usual charm and subterfuge?"

"It was the rings that did it."

"I suggested wine and roses, dinner and conversation. Just what have you done now?"

"Matching rings. Kind of like wedding bands, if you must know. Heavy carved gold by Gucci."

"And I missed the ceremony," he sighed. "Show me yours," he insisted.

"If I must," I grinned, flashing the chunk of 18 karat gold on my ring finger. "Just in case he ever feels left out. He can look at his ring and know that I'm always there for him and he must always be there for me."

"That's so sweet, I think I'm going to cry."

"Sarcasm will get you nowhere today. I'm on top of the world and going out to 'slay the dragon' this afternoon when I leave here."

The arrangements had been made last night – after I had been made. I've got to quit doing that. You guys reading this are going to think my life is nothing but love and sex. I do get a little work done in between.

Anyway, Andres had called Rafael, who called Mr. GoTo, and set up the meet. Yes, it was in that greasy, sleazy, smoky little bar on Espanola Way. The usual spot for unpleasant encounters. Andres was my backup but Rafael refused to go with us. Cited his heavy load of homework. I'll bet! The coward!

Andres arrived at the office at 1:00 PM precisely. We bid adieu to Isabel who had come in to take over for the afternoon shift.

"Where to, champ?" I asked cheerfully. "We driving or walking?"

"I've got it all worked out, Rick," he said firmly, guiding me down the hallway to the elevator. "The car is 'stashed'. Is that the word they use in the movies?"

I nodded in wonderment, who was this fellow beside me?

"We'll walk to the meet. I'll cover you from outside, across the way from the front entrance. You be out in less than thirty minutes or I call the cops."

I was astounded.

"Anything goes wrong and we have to make a run for it, the car is on the second level of that city parking garage on 17th street, across from Miami Beach City Hall."

I turned to him in amazement. "The place behind Starbucks," he confirmed, noting my confusion and thinking I had lost my way in this dizzying world of South Beach.

"Just who are you? And what have you done with my Andres?"

He grinned in shy complicity to my little jokes.

"You one of the 'Hardy Boys'?"

Now he gave me the look of incomprehension.

"I'll explain later," I grinned, thoroughly charmed by this new self-confident, take-charge kind of guy. Was it the rings that did it?

A brisk walk south from Lincoln Road on Washington Avenue took us directly to the entrance of Espanola Way, a charming re-creation of a little Mediterranean village, and the site of many movies and TV shows. Not so edgy looking in broad daylight.

But the place we were headed for was anything but cheerful. I left Andres seated at a sidewalk table, nonchalantly sipping an iced tea, while I pushed through the dirt-stained doorway of the El Morro Bar and Grill. A sense of foreboding followed me into the doom and gloom of the smoke-filled interior. I should have devised an exit plan, but time was of the essence. We needed this confrontation done quickly to get on with our case.

He was across the room, back table by the swinging door to the kitchen. Not very private – maybe that was good. Or maybe he was ready to flee out the back if I got too tough. Standoff time, or read this as 'High Noon At the OK Corral'.

"I need information about the blonde kid – José." That was easy!

"Who you talkin' 'bout?"

"The one you sent on the job to Bimini. The one that you sold heroin to. The one that got killed, his body left on the beach for strangers to find!"

"Hey, lower your voice," he warned. "I got nothin' to say about nothin'!"

"You think you can get away with this?" I stormed.

"Simmer down, buddy. I been in this town before you was born. Sent here by the 'family' to watch over things and take care o' business."

"What family?" I paused. "Oh, that one!"

It was getting hot in here and I was getting into trouble, I think.

"Look, I don't care about that stuff, I care about a confused young boy. He never hurt anyone, had a bad habit, and got killed. I just need to know who did it and why. His family needs this put to rest."

"Sit down, buddy. I'll explain how things work around here."

He motioned me to the other chair across the table. I took a seat.

He told me a lot of things, some not important to our case, but some right on target. After my thirty minutes were up, I prepared to leave.

"Hey, no hard feelings," I said. "You've been upfront with me and I appreciate it. If I ever need any other info, you available?"

"Just leave me out of it, those other guys are really vicious. You just watch your own back!" he warned, dismissing me with a wave of his hand.

I took my cue and left, in a hurry.

Andres looked up and smiled as I hit the bricks outside. He started across the courtyard but I motioned him back.

Approaching his table casually, I nodded and whispered, "Plan B, wait ten minutes and head back the way we came. Meet you at the car."

I headed toward Alton Road, the long way back, hoping he'd catch the idea and return the same way we had arrived, up Washington.

Hands in pockets, I strode briskly west past the tennis courts, park, and blocks away from where we'd been. If I had a tail on me, they'd half to show sooner or later. No where for them to hide.

Andres was waiting for me at the southwest elevator to the parking garage. Nervously glancing at his cell phone, for the time I guess. Seems wristwatches are now out of date, unless they're Rolex for maximum impression.

"Rick, you had me worried," he said breathlessly as he pulled me to him with a big hug and kiss. "You said we could do this in South Beach, right?" he grinned self-consciously.

"Yeah, champ, we can do anything you want as soon as you get us out of here!"

Cocktails on the terrace was my idea, as soon as we stepped through our front door to the cool quiet embrace of home. Andres wisely chose an iced tea, but offered to fix me a Bombay Sapphire, on the rocks and with a twist. I needed it. I had plenty of news to share with him.

"It's about your friend Rafael...his real name is..."

Twenty minutes later, I had told Andres thirty minutes worth of my conversation with the GoTo guy, hereafter known as 'mob-man' in my notes. Any other designation is up to you, I'm staying away from this subject in all future writings.

Needless to say, Andres was crestfallen. He had trusted Rafael and befriended him. He had ridden back and forth to school with him, learned English from him, and actually liked him. It was all a lie. A well-placed cover for the heir-apparent of one of S.A.'s biggest money men, a banker known as, (I cannot fill this in, I hope you understand). His stock in trade was converting drug tainted money to clean money through his many banks and holding companies through-out the western hemisphere. 'Rafael' had been sent to school here in South Florida to learn the business world, English, and all things important to ease his way up the chain. Someday he would sit in his father's place at the head of the table. Enough for today!

Andres and I took an early supper and consoled each other in the privacy of our bedroom. Tomorrow he would treat Rafael as if nothing had ever happened. Perhaps he would gradually distance himself, maybe even change schools. F.I.U. Might be a fitting choice at this point. The matter of Jose's death could now be filed under 'cold-case files' as far as I was concerned. My love and protection of Andres were my only priorities.

Andres y Ricardo

We slept late into the morning, I had called Bradley and advised him of our new information and our precarious situation. Andres had telephoned Rafael and feigned a migraine, just like in the movies, and apologized for not being able to give him a lift to school.

Breakfast on the terrace, just the two of us, a brisk dip in the ocean, stretching out in the warm sand afterward. Life almost seemed normal, but we'd have to proceed cautiously from now on. No risk taking, no nosing around this case at all. My book was going to be finished with an alternative ending. Bradley wasn't going to like it, but Andres' safety and my peace of mind were more important.

Chapter Twelve

Had to use my own key to get into the office. It was eerily quiet. No Bradley, no Isabel, no hot coffee waiting for me.

I set right to work in my small office off the conference room. I had a lot of things to put down in the 'written record' before Bradley started pumping me with questions. Certain things would be left out of the book, but I needed a complete recounting of everything I had learned on Tuesday. Just in case.

"Oh there you are," he greeted from the reception area. "Thought I'd get here before you."

"Good morning, Bradley," I sighed. Scrap that plan!

"You two enjoy your little holiday together yesterday?"

"Much needed, I'll tell you!"

"I take it, you 'slayed your dragon'?"

"Not exactly, more like questioned the 'dragon' then got the h--- out of his way!"

(We also edit that word, but do leave the 'h' in!)

"That bad, huh?" he said distractedly, trying to pour from an empty carafe.

"It's coffee by the cup, remember?"

"Oh, what's the use!" he fumed, sitting down across from my desk. "Kevin has left me. For good!"

I didn't see that one coming!

He poured forth the story, hitting the high points, until he was talked out and I was confused.

"He went where?"

"New York! With your friend Jaime!"

"Oh dear."

"He claimed I wasn't working hard enough on his career, just every other model that came though our doors! They got all the calls and call backs and I gave him nothing!"

"It's probably true, you know?" I offered quietly. "You've been very protective of him and not allowed him to run with the herd."

"All my fault," he moaned. "I wanted a boyfriend and a lover, not a working model for a roommate."

"A great friend of mine in Cincinnati once told me, when I had a similar experience, 'My dear, the best way to get over someone is to find a hot new one – right away'!"

(Word for word from my first amateurish attempt at writing gay fiction, 'Belvedere – Tales of the Queen City' by Rick Dalton)

"You got someone in mind?" he asked half-halfheartedly.

The rest of the morning was spent quietly by myself, writing down all of Tuesday's experiences. Bradley had mercifully returned to his office and left me to my own devices. By the time Isabel was there to relieve me, I had set everything down, locked the computer and was anxious to go home. To get back to my own true love.

"Rick, you got a minute for me before you go?"

"Of course, Isabel, what can I do for you?"

"It's about my brother, Paolo." She pushed a photo over the desk to me before continuing, "He's coming to Miami from Rio, and expects to stay with me when he gets here."

"Wow! Is he a model?"

"Sort of, but wants to start over in a new place. Take a few classes to improve his English, you know."

"And what's the problem?"

"He can't stay with me." She lowered her voice before continuing, "My boyfriend lives with me. My family wouldn't approve, very old fashioned, you know. Latino families are like that!"

I took another long slow look at the photo. An idea was beginning to emerge from the fog of my over-crowded brain cells.

"I think I can find a place for him with a friend of mine," I offered.

"There's something else about him you need to know first." She really whispered this time, "He's *gay*. Just broke up with his *boyfriend*."

I nearly choked on that one. The fog cleared, it was full speed ahead!

"I know exactly where he can stay! May I borrow this photo for awhile. I have to check with this friend first, he's one of those GWM's."

"*Guy with money?*" she asked innocently.

"Yes and no, but also *gay white male*. Perfect situation. His roommate just moved out yesterday."

"Thanks, Rick, I appreciate anything you can do. He gets in tomorrow. I have to pick him up at the airport. This is a real emergency."

"Leave it me," I grinned. "It's in the bag!"

After closing my office, tucking the photo in my computer case, I marched down the hallway to a door marked: Bradley Publications. You can guess who's office this is, and let myself in.

An hour later, I was out the door. Didn't take much to convince Bradley that this was the answer to his prayers. An out-of-work model, with ambitions for self-improvement, a sterling character reference from his sister Isabel, and it was not lost on either of us that he could have passed for Bradley's son. However, neither of us wanted to mention that out loud, especially the 'son' part.

"Isabel, it's all taken care of. He can stay with Bradley, our boss. He's got four bedrooms in that penthouse and three of them are empty at the moment."

"Oh, Rick, that's wonderful!' she gushed. "Thank you so much for helping out on this."

"My pleasure!" I passed the photo back to her with this suggestion, "I'd put that up on the model wall right away. He's bound to get a good job soon with his marketable looks."

A collage of photos went up on our 'model wall' immediately, Isabel was as anxious for him to get to work as she was to keep him out of her own apartment. I hoped Bradley was ready for this...

Andres looked depressed and preoccupied as I slipped through the front door our condo. He fairly jumped when I spoke out.

"Rick! Sorry I didn't hear you come in."

"Anything wrong, baby?" I teased. "Got a new lover stashed in the bedroom?"

I really shouldn't say things like that, but he needed a jolt, or a good strong cup of coffee. He appeared wan and pale, out of sorts for him.

"Can I get you a Blue Mountain to perk you up?"

"It's nothing really," he sighed. "Rafael didn't meet me down at my car this morning to ride to school, and he hasn't answered his cell phone all day."

"I'm sure there's a reasonable explanation. After all, you called out sick yesterday. Everybody has those times once in a while."

"Guess you're right. A hug and kiss would help right now."

He literally pushed me back onto the smooth black leather of our sofa and covered my body with his. I'd have to remember what I said to deserve such manhandling. I loved it!

We canceled the coffee, lunch, and dinner!

Late night sandwiches filled our hollow places as we drifted out onto the darkness of our ocean front terrace. Even the moon was lazy this evening, a no-show.

"You surprise me more and more each day," I whispered, as I held him tightly in my arms.

"That's just the beginning," he promised, "now that we really belong to each other."

A dawning light appeared, "You mean the rings?"

"Yes, baby, since we can't really be married, it shows our relationship to the whole world."

"But we *can* be married, even the President said so."

"Remember what you told me about those pieces of paper? We have our commitments to each other, the documents don't really matter."

"I guess you're right, but if you change your mind, I'll get down on me knees and propose."

"You can still do that. I'm not stopping you," he chuckled. "And while you're down there..."

Morning came all too soon, I felt like we'd gone on a second honeymoon. Come to think of it, did we have a first? Who's counting?

"Love of my life, if your car-pool buddy doesn't show today, we'll ask around. Make sure he's okay."

"Thanks, Rick. Now forget about that and help me get ready."

For what? Oh! Sometimes it takes me awhile to wake up and tune in.

"Good morning, boss!" I greeted cheerily, as I sailed in to the office. "You don't look so good."

"Thanks! I was busy cleaning house, because of you."

"Thought you had a maid for all that stuff, GWM!"

"What?"

"Never mind."

"Isabel is bringing him here directly from the airport, you know anything about that?"

"Of course. I set it all up for you. She was in a tough spot. Can't have him at her place with the boyfriend. You were in that big grandiose marble-floored condo filled with Italian designer white leather, all alone, with *no* boyfriend."

"Rub it in!"

"Look, Bradley, I only meant the best. You can look on it as helping out a friend that's in a tough spot. If the guy doesn't work out, well, fix him up with one of your rich high-class friends looking for a houseboy. Simple."

"What if I fall for the guy?"

"There's a big age difference so you'd best treat him like a son. Keep it all business, nothing personal." I paused, then added, "Unless the magic happens. This is the 'Magic City'!"

"Who's age are you referring to? Remember who writes the checks around here!"

"Lighten up, it's only nine o'clock. Let me get you a cup."

I just love poking fun at Bradley, he's such a serious guy sometimes.

He returned to his own office, down the hall. To get away from me, I suppose. I began to work on finding Rafael – for Andre's sake as well as for my case. He was looking guiltier all the time for complicity in Jose's death. The money part, I just couldn't understand. The fake note, maybe.

My calls returned no results. No one new who I was talking about. I tried using his real name with the college registry office. No results. His cell did not answer even with an anonymous call – you know the star 69 thing. I gave up just in time.

"Rick, I want you to meet my baby brother – Paolo!" Isabel gushed as she swept into the office.

Oops! Bradley was really going to be put through the test on this one – looked like a home run! Glad I don't like blondes.

(I've started a fresh page for this photo, it's needs space to breathe!)

(...or maybe that's me that needs space to breathe. I'd better hurry this along and get home to Andres before I lose my sense of propriety...)

I went straight home after escorting Paolo down the hall to Bradley's office. I had other things to worry about now – like finding Rafael.

Andres was already at home when I got there.

"I'm so glad to see you," I whooshed, sweeping him into my arms.

The startled look, followed by the pleasurable smile was my reward for being in love with Andres. You know what I mean!

After the dust settled and we exchanged our tidbits of info gleaned throughout our separate mornings, I broached the subject of Rafael.

"I can't find him anywhere, he's off the radar somehow," I began. "Maybe he's just waiting for the José matter to settle itself."

"I miss him," Andres added sadly, "he's become like a big brother to me."

We sat in silence. There was nothing else we could do at the moment. Dinner preparations commenced.

Working side by side in the kitchen, we exchanged occasional glances, elbows touched, but the matter of Rafael hung between us like an invisible curtain.

"This really means a lot to you, doesn't it?" I prodded.

His glance told me everything.

After dinner, with coffee's on the terrace, Andres snuggled next to me as unseasonable cool breezes pushed in to the shoreline.

"Rick," he began slowly, "you know how much I love you. You *are* my best friend as well as my lover, my partner."

Uh-oh!

"It's nothing to do with us, our lives together couldn't be any more perfect. It's just that … everyone needs a …"

"A Bradley!" I finished for him. "An alternative confidant, to tease, to laugh with, to pal around with – when your LTR's not available."

"Exactly. Rafael was like my older brother Eduardo, nothing more, nothing less."

"Whew! I thought you were trading me in on a younger model."

"I couldn't do that, I like the classics best of all!" he grinned.

Now what did that mean? I think the college education was going to his head, and I loved it. My Andres was going to be alright in this world I shared with him.

Chapter Thirteen

"The Murano? You're sure? When did he say this?" I probed.

"On his cell when we were driving over the causeway to school. He sounded really upset."

"Geez, no wonder he chose South Pointe Park that night he brought José to meet us."

I was pondering this new information as I lingered over my first cup of Blue Mountain Andres was rushing around to get ready for school. We had overslept. Again. Love does that sometimes.

"I'll check on it as soon as I get to work. Bradley's got friends in the real estate business. They can get us in the building, I think."

"What did you say, baby?" he stepped out of the bathroom.

"We'll go sleuthing in the building when you get back home."

"We can do that?" he called over his shoulder as he disappeared back into the steamy shower.

He was late running late, I let it pass. I didn't dare go in after him, he'd never get to school, I'd never get to work! Whew! Self-control is a b---- sometimes!

(edit the 'b' words too, except for 'B', he writes the checks!)

'Bradley - got a lead - need your advice, whenever,' I IM'd to the boss from my office computer the minute I walked into my office.

Then he walked through the door into the reception room.

"That was fast, got my message?"

"What message?"

"Never mind. I need you to get me into the Murano this afternoon."

"For?"

"To buy a new condo, ostensibly."

"You're not happy with the one I found for you two?"

"We're looking for traces of our number one suspect. I think Rafael may live there. And...he's seemingly disappeared."

"Seemingly?"

"Am I going to fast for you this morning? You need a cup first?"

"It's just that your mind is already racing to a conclusion before I even get to the starting line. Let's go from the beginning, shall we?"

We did. I filled him in on everything I knew, suspected, or wanted to find out about.

"And your new roommate?"

"What?"

"Paolo."

"Oh, you jumped ahead again."

"I do that sometimes. My stock in trade – go for the gold!"

He left the office shaking his head. Guess I was a little tough on the guy, embroiling him in one mystery after another, then thrusting a new boyfriend into his life.

And Later:

"Marcy will meet you at the Murano at two o'clock today."

"Thanks, old chum. What did you tell her I was looking for?"

"Bigger."

I'm not touching that one!

"Thanks, Andres and I will check it out, fill you in later."

I clicked off the call and finished my notes on the case. Had to write as I go on this one or details would surely get lost.

And Much Later, at home:

"Walk or ride?" I asked Andres as we settled in with a cold raspberry tea on the terrace, waiting for our appointment with the realtor.

"I think we should walk, Rick. If Rafael is there and doesn't want to see us..."

"You're right, keep a low profile until we find out what's going on."

We sipped our tea and stared at the ocean, waiting. His hand brushed against mine, found my fingers and held on tight.

"I'm sorry I got us into all this," he sighed. "We should have said no to Rafael at the very beginning."

"He was your friend. You do things for friends without question – sometimes."

"*You* are my best friend, lover, soul mate, and LTR," he confirmed, displaying his golden symbol of our commitment for each other, "and please don't ever forget that."

This could have led to...you know where, but if we were walking to our appointment, we had to leave now. So we did.

"Marcy so good to see you again," I greeted smoothly, even if a bit out of breath from the brisk half-mile walk.

"You're not happy with the one I sold you?" she asked curiously.

"We love the one we're in, thanks to you and Bradley for finding it for us. However, we were looking to perhaps upgrade to a newer building with a few more amenities, perhaps like this one."

"You've been here before?" she pursued, as a well-informed realtor is a better armed salesperson.

"We heard about it from an acquaintance."

"Oh yes, word of mouth is our best friend here in South Beach. This upscale market is really booming. The best places disappear fast."

I turned to Andres with a wink to show my intention of pulling a fast one.

"We're looking for something like our friend Rafael lives in. It may be listed under his family name, _____ ."

(I won't even include the first letter of that name, way too much info for this story, dangerous, too!)

"Let me check in with management, they'll give me the floor-plan and number of rooms, but that's about it. A privacy issue you know."

"Yes, of course. We'll just wait out here if you like."

"No, come on inside with me, have a seat in the lobby, or look over the public spaces. You will just love what they have to offer!" she enthused.

"I'll bet on that," I whispered to Andres as I steered him over to the chair grouping in the lobby. I did want to see where she went and who she spoke to.

The whole place exuded a sense of luxury, privilege, and privacy. Perfect hideaway for a person like Rafael, a young guy on the prowl with a wealthy, if somewhat notorious, father to support him.

Marcy emerged from the management office within a few minutes, a folder in her hand and a dubious look on her face.

"That very unit is up for sub-lease or sale, fully furnished, turnkey. You didn't know your friend had moved out?"

I glanced at Andres and nodded, confirming what I had already suspected – Rafael had flown the coop!

"Well, what a coincidence," I replied. "We're not really that close, just met a few times at gatherings through the modeling office."

"Oh! Okay, shall we go up and take a look then? The elevator over here will take us up to the fifth floor." She glanced at me, recalling something before continuing, "You do prefer the lower floors if I remember correctly?"

"Yes," I nodded with a grin, "heights and I are mutually exclusive."

We wandered through the elegant space of #5--, peering into closets, checking the built in cabinetry of the kitchen and pantry areas. Nothing personal remained. No remnants of the life of Rafael could be found. Even the small collection of books on a table by the bed were innocuous. The place had been cleared out and re-staged for the lease or sale.

"One thousand and eight square feet, priced at 725,000., if you decide to buy," she informed us. "Personally, Rick, not to kill a potential sale, but you have a better deal where you are – directly on the ocean and not the bay. Yes, a little older, no restaurant or concierge on duty, but I will make you money on it when you do sell. That's a promise. But for now, I suggest you hold on a bit longer until the market bounces back, then we'll upgrade you and make some money for you as well!"

"You're right on target as usual, Marcy. I've heard that said before from other friends. The market will correct itself and things will adjust accordingly."

I turned to Andres with a grin, "Alright with you, champ, if we turn this one down and do the waiting game?"

"Of course, Rick, I trust you to make those decisions."

We followed Marcy back down to the lobby and outside.

"Can I offer you guys a lift back home? I'm just on my way to the next appointment."

"That's not necessary, but thanks. I think we'll wander over to Big Pink on the way back home and catch the early bird special for supper."

She slipped into the driver's side of the white Towncar parked in the circle out front of the building and waved goodby as she sped off to her next destination.

Andres and I walked on in mutual silence through the slanting sunshine of late afternoon. Our next stop, the diner on the corner of Collins Avenue and Second Street. Coincidentally, it was the very spot where Andres and I as a couple had first met up with Rafael. A good place to put this matter to rest, once and for all, I hoped.

As the place appeared a bit crowded for this time of day, I could see the privacy factor slip away. Perhaps discussion could wait until we got back home. We'd enjoy a light meal and try to forget the case for awhile. My chief priority is always Andres, and I do want to make him happy...

Chapter Fourteen

I tossed the letter on the conference table in front of Bradley.

"What's this, another love letter from one of your clients?" he joked.

"Not exactly. Call it an explanation of sorts, or a temporary end to our case perhaps?"

"But it's addressed to Andres!"

"Of course, Andres was our only link and Rafael's friend, or so we thought. This was waiting in our mailbox yesterday when we came home from the condo search. "

Bradley studied the letter in silence. I poured coffee, my third cup for the morning. The other two with Andres before we both left home, each with our own take on Rafael's writings - or printings, shall I say.

"I'd call it a dead issue," Bradley said, looking up from the table.

"At the very least a dead end."

"You buying a new place?" he ventured, the pursing of lips and steepling of the fingers a good sign that the letter was now a moot point to him.

"Can't afford it on what you pay me," I grinned. "Three quarters of a million for the one bedroom we looked at is a trifle out of our range."

"Just why did you go looking? Thought you liked the ocean view?"

"Bradley, we discussed this yesterday. You knew we were going there to find out what happened to Rafael. A little snooping in his building. We never suspected we'd get to see the actual unit he lived in."

"Oh, that's right."

"Is everything all right with you? You seem...distracted."

"Now that you mention it...there is something. Something I suspect, but have no proof of at the moment."

"Such as?"

"The new roommate you foisted on me."

"Foisted?" I grinned again.

"I think he's using drugs."

Bradley explained a few things that I did not know about Paolo. I had only spent about ten minutes with the guy before I dropped him at the office.

"What should I do, I might be wrong about this whole thing?"

"The South Beach Boyz are now in session."

Raised eyebrows from Bradley.

"Andres and I, you and Paolo, will have a night on the town – South Beach club style," I laughed. "He's been anxious to drag me to one of the clubs ever since I first mentioned Twist and Score and all the other haunts."

"Andres is into the club scene?"

"No, he thinks I need a little diversion in my sedentary lifestyle, and this will give us all a chance to know Paolo better and see if he attempts a hook-up at the club for drugs, not boyfriends," I grinned in complicity.

We left things on hold until I could get final approval from Andres!

After Bradley had gone down the hallway to his own office at Bradley Publications, I studied the letter on the desk one more time. I wasn't really ready to call this case closed until I had a few things confirmed.

Rafael's letter claimed he had put the whole five thousand dollars and the note into the envelope before José had disappeared and before he was found lifeless on the beach. If that were the case, why that much money and why even broach the possibility of suicide? Sounded like a pre-emptive strike to me!

He must have known José would be 'eliminated' permanently and felt the guilt about to settle on his shoulders because...he knew it was going to happen and who was going to do it. An attempt to divert attention away from himself and his 'family' connections.

After all, 'family' comes first in the Latin community as well as that other one in New Jersey and New York. Rafael had been trained to prepare himself for his future role as head of this family of his. He was going to be one ruthless character when he got there!

I hadn't seen this much primp and prep since the week we were in Lima, Peru. Andres in his black leather pants, black silk shirt, chunky gold bracelet from JuanCarlo, and the Gucci gold band from yours truly! Me in, well, the usual preppy style – can't shake it.

Bradley was picking us up out in front of our building with the rental Black Lincoln Towncar he kept on retainer by the month for entertaining his o-o-t clients. It was only six blocks to the first club on our list but … appearances are everything!

Shades on, we exited the car at the front entrance of Twist on Washington Avenue, our first stop on the whirlwind tour for Paolo watching! The driver would circle out of the area and be on call when time was ready for the next stop.

Bradley was well-known at these establishments, being not only in the modeling agency business but in the publication of his gay oriented night-life magazine, 'Southern Exposure'. We were whisked past the waiting line and in the door with the most cursory of glances at our I.D.'s. Let the Paolo watching begin!

Actually, Paolo and Andres looked very much alike tonight - all dressed in black, same hair style, and same youthful enthusiasm. Color of the hair the only difference, not to mention Portuguese vs. Spanish.

For the uninitiated gay traveler, I will explain the layout of Twist. The first floor is a friendly neighborhood sort of hangout for the guys to sit and watch the door – hoping the next entrant will be their dream man personified. The stairway to the second floor leads to casual seating, standing, mixing, dancing, you name it. Back on the ground level a short hallway past the restrooms leads to other rooms and lounges, where drag shows, dancing, and other intimate contact is the norm. I think you might guess that this was not the best venue to keep track of anyone. I was depending on Andres to stick like glue to our young charge Paolo while we more sedentary types (yes, that includes you, my dear Bradley) observed the swirling masses of hot young flesh in fashionable finery cruising each other.

As the evening wore on and I wore out, we hit most all of the highlights of South Beach's gay nightclub venue. To list them here would be superfluous, as they come and go like the very surf and sand upon which we live and work. I arranged for Bradley's driver to deposit me and Andres back at our sanctuary, while the other two charged on into the nightlife of South Beach and Miami. I fully expected Bradley to call in sick on the morrow!

"Did you discover any secret passions in our dear young Paolo?" I asked as we were whisked up to our floor in the condo elevator.

"He likes men, music, and Miami," he grinned in return. "And in that order."

"No drug deals?"

"Not that I could see. We really got along pretty well considering he's on the hunt for a man and I'm not," he smirked.

"Oh ... you've found one already?" I shot back with a smile.

"Yes, and I'm about to pounce on him right now and rip his clothes off if we don't get in the door in a hurry," he threatened.

We did ... and he did! More tomorrow as my world turns...

Chapter Fifteen

And so he did! Or is that didn't? Come to work the next morning. I was all alone in the modeling office and he hadn't shown up at his publishing office...hmm. But not to worry, a pale, wan, and somewhat disheveled Bradley appeared by 12 noon, just in time for lunch.

"Care to join me?" I queried, as he slid into a seat opposite me at the conference table, my usual lunch spot on non-busy business days.

"I couldn't eat or drink anything all morning," he croaked weakly. "And I misplaced my charge."

"Your credit card?"

"My tenant."

"I think you'd better start from the beginning."

"Club Space. That's where we were – last I remember anyway."

"The very beginning," I insisted, "not the last you remember." A pause and then, "Danish with those little raisins to pick on?"

"What?" he stammered, looking seriously drawn, wan, and washed out.

"Let me get you a soda," I offered as I scooted out from my seat at the table. "That always helps me when I overindulge."

To cut to the chase (he'll probably edit out this part anyway), they exhausted every gay bar in South Beach, then headed for Miami.

Seems Paolo had a serious appetite for dancing, drinking, and the rest I'll leave to your imagination. Bradley retired to the back seat of the Towncar for a quick snooze while the driver waited in front of the club for Paolo to wear out and come out. He never did.

"Bradley, how many times have I told you to pick up your toys and put them back in the toy chest before you take your snooze?" I kidded wickedly.

"Oh, enough already! Just find him. Please."

"Since you put it that way," I smirked, "I'll get right on it. Shall I call this one 'The Case of the Missing Model' ?"

I waited until Bradley was calmed and full of ginger ale before I shooed him back to his own office, down the hallway. There's some inquiries best left for the complete privacy of my office – with the door firmly shut.

"Calvin, it's me, Rick," I began, with a call to the Miami-Dade County morgue. "Any dead young men turn up last night in the vicinity of South Beach or Club Space?"

"No young men, nothin' even close."

"Well, thanks for checking. We've got a missing wanna-be model unaccounted for. Thought I'd think the worst and start with you."

"Only one we got from over your way was a middle-aged guy found in an alley off Washington."

"Not even close, thanks Calvin."

"Funny thing about it, Rick. This guy may have overdosed on heroin like your other model – that young guy they found on the sand behind your place."

"Really?" I paused, thinking back to everyone remotely connected with Jose's death. "No I.D.?"

"A couple of gold chains, a roll of cash, no wallet or drivers license."

"Well, if you get anything else on it, let me know. I'll ask around, see if anything turns up over here."

"Thanks, Rick. You get any info, talk to Devereaux at the MBPD, he's working it."

Groan, groan! Him again!

I went back to work. Couldn't get my mind off the dead body as I cruised through the list of club managers and their private phone numbers. Nothing for Club Space. Bradley used to keep up on all the clubs, good for the modeling game and good for the magazine.

Just as I was about to call their main number from a print ad in one of Bradley's magazines – an expired issue of 'Southern Exposure' from last year, he came charging back through the office door.

"He just called from downtown Miami, he's at some motel on Calle Ocho."

"Certainly narrows it down!" I sputtered in exasperation. "It's only about as long as Miami-Dade County is wide, from Brickell Avenue to Krome Avenue. Should only take us about three weeks to check each motel or hotel on that street!"

"I did say downtown, that should narrow it a bit," he retorted defensively. "And he mentioned 'estrella', I think that's 'star' in Spanish."

"I thought he was from Brazil. They speak Portuguese."

If looks could kill, I'd be dead by now. He tossed a set of keys across the conference table.

"You drive, I don't think I can make it," he mumbled as fled for the restroom.

After much moaning and groaning, another ginger ale from our cooler, we locked up both offices and strode down Lincoln Road toward the city parking garage.

"I usually walk, but this morning I knew I'd never make it on foot all the way from home," Bradley explained as we retrieved the car.

"Did your 'charge' mention anything other than estrella?"

"He did mumble something else."

"Perhaps, 'estrella brillante'?"

"Sounds like it. You know the place?" he queried with an odd look.

"The Star Bright Motel is down that way, on Eighth Street near Miami Avenue."

He glanced over with a questioning look.

"It charges by the day or by the hour," I continued. "Like a 'hooker hotel'."

"And you know this – how?"

"I just know these things, it's part of my detecting job."

"Hmm," he murmured, with a suspicious stare in my direction. "I don't think I need to know anymore. He's in big trouble and he's going to have to go somewhere else to live. I won't have that going on in my home."

We cruised on in silence, the big elegant BMW 760Li slicing through the midday traffic in quiet elegance.

"You ever think about calling your former friend, now that you're dumping Paolo on the street?" I asked.

"Who's dumping him? He's just got to mind the house rules."

I grinned to myself, withholding the chuckle. Bradley's bark is way worse than his bite.

As we headed South on Miami Avenue and swung East on SW 8th Street, a bedraggled Paolo stood back in the shadows of the building, eagerly scanning the street. I eased over to the curb as Bradley fussed with the door handle.

"Hold up, Bradley, we can't stop in the middle of the traffic lane. I've got to pull into the parking lot or your beautiful new car goes to Mr. Braman's body shop."

"Make it quick, I don't want to be seen parking here at a prostitutes hangout!"

"I told you not to get those personalized license plates," I grinned. "Everybody knows your name."

The trip back was without incident. Bradley ignored our passenger. Paolo silently stared out the window from the back seat. I kept my eyes on the road, my mouth shut. For now at least.

I dropped them off at the front entrance of the condo building and handed the keys over to the valet.

"I'll check in at the office, make sure everything's okay and see you guys tomorrow," I called out as I turned toward the street and walked toward Lincoln Road Mall.

Thinking positive thoughts, I knew Bradley would get over it.

Between the walk to the office, a call back to Calvin at the morgue, and a different bus schedule at this later time of day, I was last getting home. Andres was already bustling around the kitchen fixing our late afternoon lunch as I pushed through the front door.

"You must have been very busy today," he chided. "You always beat me home."

"It was a long and eventful morning," I apologized and explained the activities of my day, leaving out the nature of the 'motel' where we found our missing model, Paolo. Andres didn't need to hear that part, but he did need to hear what I found out from my callback to Calvin.

"That creepy character from the bar on Espanola Way was found dead last night. Overdosed. Same as José."

We consumed our BLT's on twelve-grain toast (whoever knew there were twelve grains?) with icy glasses of Miami's version of Jamaica's raspberry tea. Sorry you asked?

Andre went first with, "What do you think that means?"

"Same method, same drug, same killer. Whoever did in José, did in the sleazy guy."

Andres' wheels were turning as he thoughtfully looked out to sea from our glass wall facing the Atlantic. Finally he turned back to me.

"You think Rafael knows who did it?"

"I think someone Rafael knows is tying up loose ends. The sleaze man probably silenced José, and now 'the family' took care of José's killer."

"You think we're in danger?" he pushed further.

"Not from Rafael, he's your friend, but from his family in drug and money laundering business, or that other family from up North – maybe?"

We sat in silence a few minutes, each staring out at the water, I finally got up from the table and drew Andres into my arms, hugging him close, wishing this was all over, and we were somewhere else – anywhere but Miami Beach.

A somber Rick entered the modeling office at an early hour. Much easier to make a few important calls, do a little thinking, planning, and trying to come up with a solution before the day's activities began.

Calvin was on duty early at the morgue. He had no more information than he did yesterday about the dead body, other than the ID had been made and the method of death was confirmed, unofficially, and off the record. He suggested I give Detective Lt. Devereaux a call at the Miami Beach Homicide Unit. Just what I didn't want to hear.

The lieutenant was in, but didn't want to give me any information. He suggested if I knew anything, I needed to come by and make an official statement, otherwise – goodbye!

Real accommodating guy, just the kind you wouldn't want to share a foxhole with.

Bradley was next through the office door. Somewhat more relaxed than yesterday, but not exactly cheerful – yet.

"Danish and coffee?" I offered. "I need your advice."

We sat across from each other at my desk instead of the big table in the conference room. More intimate and private in case any new business walked in the front door. I avoided the Paolo subject altogether and went straight for the kill (odd that I should think of it that way... or... maybe not!).

"Bradley, do I have any vacation time coming? We need to take some time out. Just me and Andres. Somewhere private, safe, and out of South Florida."

He studied me a moment before answering, "Of course, if you must get away and relax, we'll handle things here for you. I'll use this office in the morning until the secretary gets here at one o'clock, then I'll do the afternoons back in my other office." He paused again, staring. "Something's up, what is it, Rick?"

I explained it all. The two deaths being similar, the possible Rafael connection through his family if not that 'other' family.

"Andres is worried, and so am I. Not about Rafael, but those other people are cold-blooded killers. They have no conscience or remorse. They might not be done 'cleaning house'. I'd as soon be far away as wait here for the other shoe to drop."

"Where would you go? South America to Andres' country? Back to the plantation in Jamaica?"

"None of the above. They could make the connection with very little digging."

He pondered again, pencil in hand, then pencil in mouth, then... "I've got just the place!"

He pushed up out of his chair and bounded out the door. It slammed noisily behind him. Was it something I said? I grinned. Leave it to Bradley to put on the theatrics and cheer me up just when I needed it the most.

By the time I was ready to leave the office, Bradley had confirmed our 'reservations', cleared my appointments, and began implementing his plan for our getaway and salvation. Now, to sell it to Andres and start packing.

This time I got home mere minutes ahead of Andres. He looked a little calmer today than he had yesterday as we had considered our possible imminent demise.

"Bradley's found us a safe house," I proclaimed. "Not too close, just far enough. And way, way, out of the way. Practically no-man's land. No one will ever find us, I hope."

"I don't drink, but I sure could use one of your Bombay Gin things you like so much," he said, dropping down onto the sofa. "On second thought, let's just have an iced tea."

"Very wise, we've got a lot to think about."

"What about school?" he pondered, more to himself than me.

"Tell them you've lost someone very close to you and need to tend to some personal affairs. People generally understand the nature of that without asking for details."

"Where are we going?" he asked, looking up into my eyes with an almost mournful expression.

"Think of it as a little vacation, a retreat. Close-by but not in this county. Bradley won't give me the details. He said pack light, close the house, and he'll pick us up after dark."

"Tonight?"

"Eight o'clock sharp. This is what you wanted, right? Somewhere safe and protected until all this blows over or gets solved – whichever way things play out."

He stood up, wrapping me in his arms, snuggling into me, sighing with relief. "As long as we're together – just you and me. That's all we need."

Dinner was short, packing was light, and we huddled on the sofa as the clock ticked away the minutes, watching the darkening of the ocean from the shadow cast by our building as we neared our imminent departure time.

Chapter Sixteen

The sleek black car slipped through the night across Florida's Alligator Alley. Destination Naples in Collier County, at least that's as much as Bradley would disclose. A few small bags were packed into the cars trunk, along with our computers, cell phones, and other essentials of twenty-first century living.

"You'll have plenty of time to write," Bradley explained, "but you'll need to disable those cell phones."

"What is this? Some spy movie?" I expounded.

"Trust me. You'll thank me later. Make calls only from a pay phone and only if it's an emergency. No emails, no other calls, no electronic communication of any kind," he warned. "I'm unanimous in this," he grinned.

"You stole that line from Mrs. Slocombe," I accused.

"She won't mind a bit," he retorted, "she passed away in 2009."

"Leave it to you to come up with the odd bit of TV trivia."

I turned to Andres seated beside me in voluminous back seat of Bradley's BMW. "I'll explain later about British comedy," I whispered.

"I presume this place has television at least, if we're denied our electronic devices?" I queried loudly to our chauffeur in front.

"I'm not sure," he mumbled. "It's way out in the wilderness. You may have to purchase a little insect repellent, snake bite kit, the usual camping gear."

"Oh dear," I sighed, "we're being marooned on a desert isle."

"Not to worry," he retorted, "we'll pull off the highway here at the Cracker Barrel and get you a late supper. Your host for the safe house will pick you up here."

"Just where the h--- are we anyway?"

"I think it's called Rattlesnake Hammock Road," he grinned in the rear-view mirror.

He was kidding, of course. Turned out we'd exited the 'Alley', as they call this section of I-75, and onto Collier Boulevard, just northeast of Naples and close to our final destination – Golden Gate Estates.

At this late hour there were very few diners, the waitresses already worn out, and Andres and I not very hungry... fear of the unknown will do that to a guy. I had coffee, black, Andres chose Materva.

"How long do we wait on this guy?" I queried rhetorically, not expecting an answer.

"He's already here," Bradley said quietly.

I glanced furtively around the big dining area, noting a few couples, but no singles.

"That big black SUV we pulled up next to in the parking lot," Bradley continued, "belongs to your host. He's transferring your luggage as we speak."

"He with the FBI, CIA, Homeland Security?" I joked.

"Something like that."

Maybe he was, I thought. Leave it Bradley to know all types.

"He used to be a model," Bradley confided in a hushed whisper as we made our way out to the car. "That's how we know each other. His name's Pete Woodburn. Be a good house guest and this will all blow over before you know it."

And he would say no more. He left us in the parking lot and sped back toward Miami.

We whisked on through the night, safely belted into the back seat, and concealed from passing traffic by dark tinted windows. Pete didn't say much, constantly checking his mirrors, checking the rear view camera screen on the center of the dash, so I held onto Andres and gazed into the inky blackness.

The morning sun streamed through the glass wall of the bedroom, as I glanced around our 'new' quarters. Andres was curled up next to me, still sleeping soundly. I eased gently out of the bed and strode over to the window. Palms, pines, oaks, tall grasses, as far as the eye could see. We were in a small clearing amidst a jungle of vegetation. The house appeared to be isolated from the rest of the world.

As I turned toward the bed, Andres was struggling out of his dream world and back to reality.

"Who's making breakfast?" he called out sleepily.

"Your chef is on the way to the kitchen, if I can find it," I declared with a bow toward my beautiful partner, as he snuggled back into the bed covers.

The house is circular, as I had noted last night on our first sight of it, after driving along a curved and rutted lane through dense underbrush. It stood in a flat clearing of low cropped grasses and slightly raised from ground level to provide parking underneath. It did not go unnoticed by me, an architecture aficionado, that it closely resembled a Frank Lloyd Wright design placed up on stilts.

A quick turn through the great room on the opposite side of the two bedrooms, revealed a circular kitchen in the exact center of the structure. A clear glass dome above lighted the small work space.

"What time is it?" Andres mumbled, rubbing sleep from his eyes as he slipped up from behind, encircling me with a good-morning hug.

"Almost noon and our host said he'd see us for a late lunch so we could sleep in."

"Looks just like back home in Ecuador, the trees and jungle, only flat. No ravine, no roaring river at the bottom of a steep path."

"Do you miss your old home?" I asked softly, with a slight frown.

"Of course not, silly. I love my life with you in our stylish condo, on the white sandy beaches along the crystal blue ocean waters."

"You writing a term paper for school or a travel brochure?" I kidded.

"Go take your shower, while I fix lunch for three if that guy's coming back here," he scolded.

I always follow Andres' suggestions, as he's usually right...and I love him above and beyond anyone and anything else.

Our lunch was served on square plates on the round dining table at one side of the great room. Pete sat with his back to the end wall of the great room while Andres and I sat opposite but still with a clear view of the vast outdoors. The view was the same as from the two bedrooms – trees, vines, tall grasses all around.

"What made you pick this spot?" I wondered aloud, as we munched on our club sandwiches, downed our iced teas, all thanks to our host for providing and Andres for creating.

"Security," he replied tersely. "I do a lot of traveling out of the country. This is convenient and off the beaten track. State-of-the-art electronics keeps it safe when I'm away on business."

"What business are you in?" I probed. "Bradley has never mentioned you before."

"Research and development, product technology, and occasionally - investigation."

"Hmm." What else could I say? He wasn't much for conversation, so we finished our lunches in relative silence.

Pete stood up to clear away the lunch dishes, while Andres and I walked out onto the gallery that curved around the outside of the living room portion of the house.

It's really beautiful out here in a wild sort of way," I grinned, "but not like our own home!"

"I agree, let's go home please," Andres urged. "We're just delaying the inevitable."

I turned to him in surprise. "Your education is paying off. Now, can you spell it?" I teased. If looks could kill, I'd be dead and buried.

We agreed to end our not-well-thought-out sabbatical and return to Miami Beach. Pete offered to drive us that very afternoon, provided that we permit him do a little electronic surveillance wiring in our condominium. A good sound recorder, cameras, silent alarms, and remote monitoring capabilities. I don't know what all that means exactly, but if it gets us back into our own home and our lives can return to a semblance of the old routine, it would be worth it.

Days, weeks, a month went by, as life went on. Andres was about to finish another term at Miami-Dade College. I was back to work in the mornings at Bradley's fashionable modeling office known as Model Solutions. And Bradley himself was back to doing whatever erstwhile publishers of books and gay-oriented magazines such as 'Southern Exposure' do.

Our experiences in fleeing our home to hide out in the wilds of southwestern Florida had solidified our relationship even more as Andres and I came to understand that we were going to make it after all. As a couple, that is. My book on the the 'missing model' had been shoved aside temporarily as there was no solution in sight as to who killed José or the sleazy character that ran the bar on Espanola Way.

The 'other shoe' finally dropped one evening. Andres' cell phone rang. It was Rafael. He was nearby and wanted to see us right away. And he wanted to be let in by the beach side private entrance to avoid being seen.

I turned on all Pete's security devices before we went down the five flights of service stairs to meet Rafael at the back door.

The one formerly known as the 'Ice Man', AKA Rafael, stood before us. Calm, cool, and impeccably dressed in the latest fashionable suit as only Armani could design it. We decided to use the elevator for our return trip to floor five – less stressing to the newly and elegantly attired mobster's son. (I may have to scratch that – Bradley, can we be sued?)

'The Ice Man' took a chair by the wall, Andres and I on the sofa. I offered drinks, Rafael declined. I had one anyway. Bombay on ice – straight up. I think I was going to need it.

"I'm leaving for Rome tonight," he began. "I think there's a few things you need to know about my sudden disappearance."

"At the very least!" I shot back.

"My father called me back home to explain his grand plans for me. I have to study abroad and get serious about this financial world he runs. I have to be his right arm until I'm ready to take over for him."

"Kind of like Michael Corleone in 'The Godfather'," I interjected.

I guess he doesn't read or watch the reruns as it went right over his head.

"What happened to José?" Andres asked. "Did you do anything to hurt him?"

"I loved him," he added simply. "I would never hurt someone I love."

"Who didn't love him then? Because somebody's killed him, made it look like a self-injected overdose of heroin. Then the sleaze bag at the bar got wiped out the same way," I interjected again.

"He was in over his head," Rafael said sadly, "way over."

We waited it out. He had to say more. The tapes were recording.

"You know how it is in some families, they don't accept a gay son. Especially one with a boyfriend living with him."

"So your 'family' had him 'iced'?" I couldn't resist that little jab.

He looked up, startled.

"We're in the banking business, not 'Murder Incorporated'."

So he does watch movies and television.

"Who do you hold responsible then?" I pressed on.

He squirmed around in his crisp new suit, running his finger around the edge of the too-tight collar as he considered my question.

"This goes no further," he began. "It's only because I care about you guys and trust you to do the right thing."

I nodded, we waited, he squirmed some more, then went on.

"My family *may* have contracted some local business through the 'Go-To' man at the bar. José got mixed up in it somehow, went to work for them to get a score – some cash for his addiction. He was staying with me back then. My father found out about it."

"So you're saying, make that *implying*, that your father had Go-To murder José because he was your gay boyfriend and for no other reason?"

"You just couldn't let it alone, could you?" he gasped.

"And who did in the sleaze-ball murderer?" I pressed on.

"That's another matter," Rafael retorted. "Those guys clean up their own messes and their own crew. Someone skims a little too much, gets careless, talks about it to the wrong people. Then somebody comes into town and retires them permanently."

Whew! That was a lot more than I bargained for. Two cases solved for the price of one.

"I got to get going," Rafael said, jumping up out of his chair. "My plane leaves tonight and I shouldn't even be here."

Andres and I both got up and followed him to the door. He turned and hugged Andres, shook my hand.

"I really do care about you two guys. I'm going to miss you both. You've been good friends through this whole thing."

I held the door open, but Andres walked him out to the elevator alone. When he returned, his eyes were glistening, ever so slightly.

As I closed the door I turned toward the living room and said loudly, "I hope you got all that, Pete, the ball's in your court now, we're out of it and I'm turning off this whole suite of electronic gadgets until you come and get it out of here!"

I held on to Andres tightly as we walked into our bedroom. We'd both been through an ordeal or two or three, but our love and understanding still holds us together as one.

A thought occurred to me as we gently closed the bedroom door. It was something I had said about Raphael months ago before we had become so entangled with him. 'Never trust a guy who wears Gucci sunglasses!'

This is a wrap! Okay, Bradley, edit out my mistakes, but don't change the words unless your attorney insists. Print!

BODY ON THE BEACH

A RICK DALTON MYSTERY

BY
RICHARD D. CLAGETT